Praise for

"Sometimes just being an observer or witness of terrible crimes carries horrendous guilt because we believe we could have done something to stop it. Author, Mary Mills, was powerless to make things better as a child. My Father's Ledger is just one way that Mary has helped to right the wrongs and show a way to peace. It is a riveting, exquisitely written and inspiring story of loss and triumph."

Mary Dispenza, Author of SPLIT - A Child, A Priest, and the Catholic Church, Northwest leader of SNAP, Survivors Network of Those Abused by Priests

"Most people we know from a distance – guarded, edited and veiled. Others, like Mary enter gently yet clearly with a powerhouse of brutal reality. Mary is the real deal. The women in her life and the stories of their lives will resonate with countless others who have been victims of sexual manipulation and injustice. She risks everything in revealing family secrets. Healing is shared in the process. Mary breaks unholy silence to give voice to the holy mystery where broken experience meets the hope of God's love. In uncovering dusty generational skeletons and connecting the dots, lies lose power. Truth brought into light births healing. In the light, in the Sole-Light of Christ the power of secrets are silenced. How grateful I am to have a friend willing to push back the dark. I'm honored to call this warrior-lady my friend. I applaud her courage. Bravo Mary Mills."

Bonnie Keen, Author, Recording Artist, Actress

"My Father's Ledger *is a powerful and sobering account of betrayal and abuse by those we are taught to trust most. Sexual abuse by clergy eviscerates lives and too often destroys precious souls. In the midst of the darkness and hopelessness, this book introduces us to a God who not only grieves with those who have been abused, but who moves towards them with an indescribable compassion. A compassion where He is so moved and overwhelmed by the distress of the wounded that their distress and pain becomes His own. My Father's Ledger is a beautiful and hopeful picture of how God's love can bring beauty out of the ashes. A much needed comfort for so many."*

Basyle, "Boz" Tchividjian: Author, Professor of Law, Founder of GRACE (**G**odly **R**esponse to **A**buse in the **C**hristian **E**nvironment

My Father's Ledger

Sex Abuse by a Catholic Priest
A Family's Story of Grace, Survival and Healing

Mary A. Mills

❃ ❃ ❃

My Father's Ledger

Sex Abuse by a Catholic Priest
A Family's Story of Grace, Survival and Healing

Legacy Builder Books

Building a Legacy of Grace

Epigraph

You have taught me since I was young, O God, and I still proclaim the wonderful things You have done. Now as I grow old and my hair turns gray, I ask that You not abandon me, O God. Allow me to share with the generation to come about Your power; Let me speak about Your strength and wonders to all those yet to be born.

God, Your justice stretches to the heavens, You who have done mighty things! Who is like You, O God?

Psalm 71:17–19, *The Voice*

Dedication

To Aunt Donna and Uncle Ray, two of the most loving and Christ-like Catholics I have been blessed to know.

And to Elsie Boudreau: were it not for her bravery, this story may have never been told.

Acknowledgements

My greatest thanks to Jesus Christ, my Lord and Savior. Were it not for Him this story would definitely have ended very differently.

To Lee, my husband, best friend and the most enduring support a woman could ever dare to hope for. You are the wind beneath my wings.

Kay and Randy Creech: Your encouragement and prayers have blessed me more than you'll ever know. Thank you for the priceless gift of your generous hospitality during the many hours of blessed retreat at your beautiful ranch. A great majority of my best work occurred there amongst the pines.

Erin Brown, Editor Extraordinaire: Thank you from the bottom of my grammar challenged heart. You are the best home school mom/editor I could have ever hoped for.

To all of my dear siblings: I can't imagine how differently my life would have turned out if not for your love, acceptance and support. I am blessed to be a member of such a diverse family of amazing individuals. I believe we have done our parents proud.

To my beautiful, perfectly flawed parents: Dad, you are beyond a doubt my greatest hero. Your example of what a good man looks like, helped me to finally find the good man I found in my husband Lee. Mom, my memories of your gentle kindness and generous spirit instilled in me a like-minded attitude toward those in need of compassion.

To my church family/Christian community, too numerous to name individually: Thank you for your interest, concern and especially your prayers – they have carried me through many dark seasons of doubt, fear and discouragement. Bless you!

To my wonderful 'Saddle Tramp' girlfriends: The fellowship of like-minded women, enjoying the beauty of God's creation from the back of a horse has proven to be my best therapy. Like they say, there is nothing better for the inside of a girl, than the outside of a horse. Thank you for sharing my equine love affair and especially thank you for enduring my countless musings along the trail, during my writing process.

To a very special Saddle Tramp friend, Luanne Bauman, who rode into the glorious beyond on October 10th 2016: Thank you Lu for believing in me and for encouraging me when I wanted to give up. You are one of my greatest heroes and I miss you more than words can express. Have a horse all saddled and waiting for me when I'm called home, okay.

My deepest gratitude goes to the following people who painstakingly read, reviewed and critiqued my early drafts. Your feedback helped tremendously. Debra Allard, Vicky Angyus, Gretchen Langton, Dan and Deb Ashmore. Thank You!

To the wonderful authors I have been honored to get to know and from whom I received much needed words of encouragement and praise: Rebecca Ondov, Bonnie Keen, Joanna Weaver, Julie Barnhill, Sue Buchanan, Angela Breidenbach, and Susan Thomas. Thank you for blazing the trail before me and for inviting me into your community of professionals.

To my Massage Therapy clients, many of whom have also become loving friends: Thank you for your interest in my work as an author and for your words of encouragement and support.

To all who faithfully read my bi-monthly newsletter, '*Building a Legacy of Grace*,' Thank you!

Contents

Author's Note

This is a true story; however, in an effort to respect the privacy of the individuals, many of the names have been changed. Though some of the conversations are not verbatim, they are as close as my memory allows. I have endeavored to relate the facts as accurately as possible.

It is with the most utmost respect that I tell my story. I wish in no way to offend any person for their Catholic faith. It is the hierarchy of the church that is being called to accountability, and it is for the faithful who have been victimized that I tell my story. May it bring healing and hope.

Preface

Babes in the Woods

My dear don't you know of a long time ago,
Two poor little babes whose names I don't know
Were stolen away on a bright summer's day
And left in the woods as I've heard people say.

And when it was night so sad was their plight.
The sun had gone down and the moon gave no light.
They sobbed and they sighed and they bitterly cried,
And the poor little babes they lay down and died.

And when they were dead the robins so red,
Brought strawberry leaves and over them spread.
And all the night- long they sang their sad song,
Poor babes in the woods. Poor babes in the woods.

Anonymous

May 1965

"Mommy, Mommy, come tuck us in!" Roseanne rubbed her eyes as she snuggled next to me. The chirping song of robins gathering their evening meal floated through the open window. A warm breeze brought with it the scent of spring blossoms and mingled with the faint spicy aroma of the evening meal that lingered in the air of our little room above the kitchen.

In my bed, the lower bunk, my sister and I were surrounded by a veritable zoo of our combined collections of stuffed animals. Having grown weary of the great adventures we had just taken them on, we were ready to settle down for the night.

Hearing Mom's footsteps ascending the stairs, Roseanne pushed against me as I slid toward the wall. We giggled and squirmed as our mother entered the room then playfully swung her hip, scooting us even closer together and toward the wall. She ducked her head under the top bunk, settling in on the edge of the bed.

"Snug as a bug in a rug." She cooed as she made mock tucking motions against the blankets. The three of us there in the evening light between the two beds made for a very cozy rug indeed.

"Sing us a song. Pa-lease." I nudged Roseanne with my elbow and Mom moved over a bit, toward the outside edge, so that we could all get comfortable.

"All right, but just one. It's getting late and you both have school tomorrow."

"Yeah, but just two more weeks, and then summer vacation—"

"Yeah, and then I can't wait for next year," Roseanne said, "'cause, I will be in Sister Damion's second grade class. She's the nicest teacher in the whole school."

"And I get to be in the *new* school building in Sister Bernadette's fifth grade class, and I think she's the nicest."

"Well, how lucky. Between you two, you will have the two nicest teachers in the whole school." Mom's comment settled the competition. "So, what shall I sing?"

"Sing 'Babes in the Woods,'" Roseanne begged.

"Yeah, yeah!" I clapped my hands. "'Babes in the Woods!'" I never grew tired of hearing the familiar words to the old song, a frequent request of our nightly bedtime tucking-in ritual.

"All right, then, close your eyes."

As she began to sing, I sighed and closed my eyes. Her voice, so soothing and gentle, filled the room and my little heart with the sweet haunting melody. Hearing it once again, I felt a dreamy sense of sorrow and safety all at once.

Roseanne snuggled closer to me, sniffing back a tear.

Opening my eyes, I studied my mother's face. She returned my gaze, and I saw that her light brown eyes, the color of hazelnuts, she'd once told me, were filled with tenderness. Her wavy auburn-tinted hair framed her delicate face and set off her high cheekbones and fair complexion, giving her an elegant look. Her lips curved into a gentle smile as she brushed my cheek with the back of her hand and continued singing.

"…And when they were dead…."

The words drifted like cool feathers across my thoughts. I shuddered slightly, feeling a breeze from the open window.

"...the robins so red brought strawberry leaves and over them spread...."

The chirp-chirp of the robins outside blended with the lilt of my mother's voice.

"...and all the night long they sang their sad song...."

Roseanne sniffed, louder this time, and snuggled even closer.

"...Poor babes in the woods. Poor babes in the woods."

My mother had a beautiful singing voice, like the voice of an angel. She loved music, as did my father. She played the piano and the guitar. Just recently I discovered she also played the mandolin. Along with one of her sisters and two of her brothers, they had formed a quartet in high school and were quite popular in the Beaverton, Oregon, area.

My father played the fiddle and the mandolin. His voice was a deep baritone, though he rarely sang. On the few occasions he did, our favorite was his rendition of "Barnacle Bill the Sailor" We loved how he would sing, "Yo, ho, ho" and then several octaves down the scale, "I'm Barnacle Bill the Sailor." It always made us kids laugh.

But mother, she loved sad songs. I guess that just went along with her melancholy personality. She sang of unrequited love, lost loves, and lost lives.

When I was a little girl, Mom was always singing or humming as she went about her daily chores. She would play the piano for hours, one song after another. She would sit with her guitar beside our record player, learning to play songs by ear from the record. I grew up on songs from the '40 s, like "Don't Sit Under the Apple Tree," "My Bonnie Lies over the Ocean," WWII love songs—the list is extensive.

But it was the sad, old-timey ballads that seemed to capture her emotions, like, "Tom Dooley," "Green Green Grass of Home," and "If I Had the Wings of an Angel." The songs were about lovers behind bars, beyond reach, or heading for the gallows. Songs of betrayal, longing, and desire.

Even the sweet song so many of us know from our childhoods, "You Are My Sunshine" with its lovely lyrics "You make me happy when skies are gray. You'll never know, dear, how much I love you" begs "Please, don't take my sunshine away." Few people know the second and subsequent verses. They speak of shattered dreams, broken promises, bargaining and begging for loyalty. One verse offers threats and curses if these promises are not secured or the dream is unfulfilled. Wow!

Concerning the song I opened this Preface with, "Babes in the Woods," it is unclear when this song was originally written, but tradition has it that an uncle, guardian of the two babes, wants their inheritance, so he hires two rascals to take them into the woods to kill them. One of the thugs kills the other, and, too tenderhearted to murder the babies, he abandons them in the woods to starve to death. Unlike Hansel and Gretel, they did not leave a trail of breadcrumbs, and no one finds them in time.

In an email sent to the Babes in the Woods Website, a visitor made this comment: "My daughter, one of six children, was put to bed each night by my singing to them. 'Babes in the Woods' was their favorite. My mother sang it to me and my siblings also. We grew up with this song. My children were so sad that the poor babes had to lie down and die that I was forced to write another ending for the song:

"And when it was light, the sunshine so bright
Shone down through the trees and warmed up the leaves.
The little babes woke and found their way home
And promised their dad, nevermore would they roam."[1]

Roseanne, and I identify so much with this song. We have both said many times how much we felt like those babes in the woods, left alone to fend for ourselves. By the grace of God we did not die (nor were we "raised by wolves," as our older siblings often tease). Roseanne summed it up perfectly when she read the Website: "No one found us in time, but God saved us and showed us the way."

Introduction
MY FATHER'S LEDGER

A few years ago I received a telephone call from my stepsister, Nancy, telling me that she had a box full of my father's personal belongings. She had been cleaning out an upstairs storage area in her home and discovered it among some of her mother's things she had saved following her death in 2003. Dad had passed away in 1994, so I was pleasantly surprised to receive these items that I had, quite honestly, either forgotten about or didn't know they existed.

When I received the box, I opened it with eager anticipation and rifled through its contents. Included were a collection of cards and letters that we (his children) had sent and he had lovingly saved. I pulled out an assortment of important documents, like Mom and Dad's marriage license, Dad's eighth grade graduation certificate from Jerome High School in Idaho. I found Mom's yearbook from Beaverton High in Oregon and even an autograph book from her classmates at Adam's High School in Omaha, Nebraska, from 1938.

I was delighted to receive these long-forgotten records and spent a quiet Sunday afternoon lingering over each precious item. Of special interest to me was a small book tucked in at the bottom of the box. I pulled it out and opened it: a ledger that began in January 1965 and its final entry dated May 1976. As I browsed through this book, I noted Dad's neat handwriting and how detailed and organized his entries were. As I scanned the pages, I thought, *How interesting that every page seems to tell the story of what was going on in our lives at the time of the entries.* There was the record of every month's tuition payment to St. Mary's of the Valley Academy and of Dad's faithful tithes to St. Cecilia's Church. Listed were payments for dancing and music lessons, Sears and J.C. Penny's, and all the usual utility companies and such. It seemed to me that he kept a record of just about every penny he spent.

Then I noticed a shift in the entries, beginning around the middle of 1966, which coincided with how our lives had changed. Added to the usual everyday expenses were entries of payments to Beaverton Ambulance Company. And instead of medical expenses that had originally included only our regular family physician and dentist, additional entries pointed to a number of specialists, which seemed to increase in number exponentially each month. *This book really does tell a story.*

I tucked the ledger back into the box, vowing to pull it out again someday and read it more thoroughly. I put the box into my storage closet and pretty much forgot about it—that is until…. Well, that's where the story really gets interesting.

✾　✾　✾

Two years after I had put Dad's ledger back into the box and stowed it safely away, I received the following phone message from Roseanne. She was in the midst of preparing for a legal settlement.

"Hey, Mary, this is Rosie. Hey, listen, I just had this thought…. I was just talking with Kelly [Rosie's attorney] on the phone and he [Kelly] said, 'I'm sitting here with your dad's ledger, looking through it, and it's very interesting. I'm going to spend some time reading through it. I'll call you later and tell you what some of my impressions are and give you some of my thoughts.'

"And I, (Rosie) started thinking about that ledger and thinking about the twenty zillion years ago, however long ago it was, Dad sitting at a table with that ledger and not knowing the journey this ledger was going to take. And how its journey has ended up in the hands of this high-powered attorney in downtown Portland. What would Dad think if he knew his ledger was sitting there being read?

"I thought of this theme and title for a book, our story. We could call it 'The Ledger.' It's kind of about justice, you know [the record] of good and evil—the balance. And of the debts and deposits and of the expenses…."

Part One

✼　✼　✼

Chapter One
GRACE: AT THE TABLE WITH THE PRIESTS

"Why would God require of us an unnatural act that defies every primal instinct? What makes forgiveness so important that it becomes central to our faith? The Gospels give a straightforward answer to why God asks us to forgive: because that is what God is like. When Jesus first gave the command "Love your enemies," he added this rationale: "that you may be sons of your Father in heaven" (Matt. 5:44–45). We are called to be like God, to bear God's family likeness.

"The gospel of grace begins and ends with forgiveness, and people write songs with titles like 'Amazing Grace' for one reason: grace is the only force in the universe powerful enough to break the chains that enslave generations. Grace alone melts ungrace."[1]

January 2009

Roseanne slowly maneuvered her Volkswagen Passat toward downtown, her fingers drumming an impatient rhythm on the steering wheel. In the front passenger seat, Beth softly hummed a little hymn in an attempt to calm us all. Wiping away a small circle of fog, I leaned my forehead against the back window, craning to see beyond the traffic stacked up ahead.

Driving the back roads from West Linn, Oregon, to Northwest Portland would normally have been much faster than the freeway. Under different circumstances, the route along Macadam Avenue was a pleasant drive: scenic and tree lined with a parallel view of the Willamette River. However, a recent snowstorm had reduced visibility, hiding the river behind a low cloud cover. And an accident had slowed the early morning commuter traffic to a near standstill.

As the line of cars inched toward downtown, the storm churned around us, and I felt a rising anxiety regarding our upcoming meeting. The weather reflected my mood—cloudy, swirling, and stuck.

I had been asking myself for days, What is this meeting about—for me? Do I have anything I want to say? I had been getting up early the past few days, spending the quiet morning hours lifting those questions in prayer. *Here I am, Lord, speak to me. Tell me what You want me to hear. Tell me what You want me to say.* My sisters Beth and Roseanne had both written out their thoughts and were very clear on what they would say. But so far nothing had come to me.

None of us were looking forward to this meeting, but we were eager to have it behind us, to move on in anticipation of the sense of closure we believed would follow.

As the emergency vehicles worked to clear the scene and the flow of traffic picked up speed, my anxiety increased further. Breathing deeply, I prayed, *God, grant me serenity.*

Beth continued humming softly, filling the car with a sense of God's presence. *He is my peace, and has broken down every wall....*

Slowly the familiar melody penetrated my mind. He is my peace, He is my peace. Ever so gradually, true to words of the beloved hymn, I felt an increasing sense of calm settle over me as I realized that even if I didn't say a word, my presence would speak volumes: a silent statement regarding the strength of our family unity.

Of the six Mueller siblings, four of us would be in attendance today: Roseanne, the youngest, Beth, our brother C.J. (Clarence Jackson), and me. The two oldest siblings, Diana and Joan, had declined to participate.

This meeting would mark the end of a two-year legal battle initiated by Roseanne, which eventually involved all of us siblings in varying degrees. Rosie had requested this time as part of the settlement agreement she had accepted three months earlier. Thank God it was almost over!

During the course of the past two years, we had revisited many painful memories and discovered long-hidden family secrets. Being asked to look into the past, nearly forty years, had affected each of us in our own way.

The most difficult thing for me had been the frustration of not being able to remember segments of my personal history. C.J. had also expressed having a similar experience of memory loss.

Beth's had been the unpleasant memory of a period of her life when significant life-changing events occurred for her, over which she had no control. That experience sent her on a journey of heartache and loss she has had to bear for most of her adult life.

I am certain that Diana and Joan have been affected in ways far deeper than we will ever know. To this day neither of them is comfortable discussing this part of our family's history.

Without a doubt, Roseanne has been most deeply affected by the evil that threatened to destroy our entire family. The evil that was greatly responsible for our mother's, Martha, untimely death.

⁂

When we finally arrived at the attorney's office, running a bit late, we discovered our brother, C.J., had arrived just ahead of us. He had already met the attorney's assistant, Jen, who greeted us then led us down the hall to a conference room.

As we entered the room I was immediately taken aback by the imposing view through the large widows that spanned the east-facing wall. The law firm is located on the west bank of the Willamette River in view of the Fremont Bridge, and although several hundred yards from the river's shore, the impression is that one could step right onto the bridge and cross to the other side.

Glancing around the room, I spotted a collection of pen-and-ink drawings and old photographs displayed along the walls that depicted several of the city's many bridges.

Jen pointed out the refreshment table that stood at the north end of the room, inviting us to help ourselves. A large oval conference table occupied the center of the room, and in the south corner was a large overstuffed chair.

As we all took a few moments to adjust to the surroundings, I observed that C.J.'s usual calm and upbeat demeanor had taken on a serious and agitated edge.

"Roseanne, where do you want me to sit?" he said.

"Anywhere you feel comfortable," she said. "I'm just so glad you're here."

"We all are," Beth and I said in unison.

"I think I'd like to just sit over there in the corner. I want to be supportive, but I'd really rather not sit at the table, by *them*, if that's okay." His voice trembled, his breath catching in a little hiccup. "I ran into them in the elevator on the way up. I'm just having a little trouble with all of this." He sniffed and struggled to retain the fragile hold on his composure.

The tension of the moment filled the room, and, without a word, we four siblings found ourselves in a spontaneous embrace. C.J. shook with emotion, his usual good humor darkened and his self-control momentarily unchecked. We remained thus, in an intimate huddle, likely only for a few seconds, yet time seemed to stop, like the freeze fame on a video, before we felt him calm.

After a few moments we pulled slowly apart, reluctant to end the moment of tenderness.

"It just took me so by surprise—running into them. I wasn't prepared for that." C.J. heaved a sigh, his voice shaking.

Closing her eyes, Roseanne shook her head. "I had no idea when I started this process that it was going to be so painful for everyone—and difficult."

"I'm sure none of us did." C.J. said. He shook his head and gave a wan smile.

Jen, who had been standing across the room at a polite distance, now stepped gingerly between our intimate group huddled near the door. As she reached for the door, she turned to Roseanne. "Keep in mind that you're in control. This is your power. This is about *you*."

"I'm there." Roseanne said, clearly resolved.

"All right then, good," Jen said, and closed the door softly behind her.

Taking another deep breath, C.J. squared his shoulders and walked toward the overstuffed chair at the corner of the room. I followed suit, pulling up a chair beside him.

In a few minutes the door opened. We all stood as the two men entered the room. Father Lee (Provincial for the NW Jesuit Society) introduced himself first then Jim Poole, aka Father Poole, a retired Jesuit priest.

The awkward introductions complete, Roseanne directed the two priests to the chairs directly opposite hers, and we all took our seats. She thanked them for coming then began the meeting by stating that she had written what she wanted to say in order to stay on track.

Roseanne cleared her throat.

I observed how Father Lee sat with his head tilted slightly down and toward Roseanne as she read. He placed his folded hands, palms down on the table in front of him, listening politely, with apparent discomfort.

Jim Poole, however, sat with his hands clasped tightly in his lap. He sat erect, eyes straight ahead, staring unblinking just over Roseanne's right shoulder, as though he were looking into some great expanse behind her. He then began to slowly twirl his thumbs, rhythmically. One over the other.

I studied him closely. Questions came unbidden. *Is this truly the same man who had so deeply affected all of our lives? The once charming, handsome, and charismatic persona that had bewitched us all? This benign-looking, eight-two-year-old grandfatherly-looking man, slightly stooped, with a slow and somewhat shuffling gate? Could it really be this man who was responsible for causing such destruction and misery in the lives of so many? Did he have any sense of regret or affection when he thought of our beautiful mother, Martha, or was she just one among the multitude of his exploits?*

Jim continued his hypnotic thumb twirling as Roseanne began to read, her voice slow, steady, and calm. "I would like to begin today by saying that I don't have any expectations for either of you to make any kind of statement or apology to me. In fact, I would almost prefer that you didn't try to say anything to appease me. I would also like to say that I prefer not to refer to you as Father Poole; I will refer to you as Mr. Poole.

"That said, I will introduce myself. I am Roseanne Miller, and my maiden name is Mueller. My mother was Martha Mueller, a woman whom you befriended in 1965 when you came to Oregon. My father was Clarence Mueller.

"I have two reasons for requesting this meeting today. The first is to remind you, Mr. Poole, since you claim to have forgotten, about my family and your involvement with us. I want to let you know the sequel of what happened in our lives after you went back to Alaska and carried on your work of damaging the lives of countless other women and children."

As Roseanne continued to read with her voice strong, confident, and amazingly calm, I wondered just how much he remembered. What kind of lasting impression did his involvement with our family leave in his memory? Surely he remembered our mother. But the biggest question in my mind was, would he, after being confronted in this way, finally admit it?

As Roseanne continued to address her written thoughts directly to the two priests, my heart swelled with pride at the strength and clarity of her words. I listened intently, though my attention was momentarily drawn once again to the view out the expansive windows, and I wondered where life might take us after we crossed this massive bridge we were traveling today.

Chapter Two
THE DINNER GUEST

October 1964

"Hey, Mom, what's for a snack?"

As Roseanne and I stomped through the front door, I gave my sister a hearty shove, jockeying for first position into the house. Our bare legs, under our school uniforms, were chapped, numb, and red from the chilly fall wind that whipped against us on our walk home from St. Mary's of the Valley Academy for Girls. The school was a little over two miles from our house and the walk always worked up a huge appetite.

"Close the front door. You'd think you were both born in a barn." Mom's voice coming from the back of the kitchen contained a playful, lighthearted firmness I hadn't heard for some time.

The savory aroma of a pot roast stirred an even deeper hunger pang, and I jostled my sister toward the door, determined to get to that longed-for snack before her. "You were last in, so you close it."

"No I wasn't. You were," she resisted with a stubborn, chin in the air, arms across her chest defiance.

This was just one of our many familiar arguments. "It's your turn." (Or my turn, if it was to my advantage.) "You're on my side." "She got more than me." "It's not fair." And on and on it would go, an endless variety of arguments and defensive postures.

"Well, neither of you will get a cream puff if that door isn't closed in the next thirty seconds."

The ensuing race to the front door sounded like nothing short of the tromping of a small herd of elephants.

Typical of most siblings, Roseanne and I alternated between being best friends one minute and mortal enemies the next. But one thing we've never argued about was that our mother's cream puffs were out of this world. It almost hurt just looking at them. They were so beautiful. Filled with fluffy whipped cream or sometimes with gooey rich chocolate, lemon, or vanilla pudding, and most often crowned with a glorious drizzle of sweet chocolate glaze.

Coming home to find a tray of these delectable delights chilling in the refrigerator was a little glimpse of heaven.

"What's the special occasion?" I inhaled the savory aroma of the pot roast I spied through the oven door. Cream puffs and pot roast were usually reserved for company or a special day like Easter or birthdays. As far as I knew, today was just an ordinary Wednesday.

"As a matter of fact, we are having a special guest for dinner tonight," Mom said as she presented a cream puff on a little saucer she had reserved for Rosie and me. "You girls will have to split this one. I made only so many, and, besides, I don't want you to spoil your appetite."

"Oh, Mom, can't we have our own?" I said in my sweetest tone. "I'm starving!"

"No, just a half for now, but you can each have a whole one after dinner. Now, who is going to cut this?"

The rule was that one of us would cut whatever we were to share and the other got to choose the half, a guaranteed way to ensure that the one with the knife be very exact.

"So, who's the company?"

"Yeah, who?" Rosie echoed as she watched me ever so carefully place the knife in the precise center of the lusted-after snack. Whipped cream oozed out of the top and around the sides as it yielded to the knife. With my forefinger and thumb I carefully stripped the mixture of whipped cream and chocolate glaze from the blade. Eyeing Roseanne I sucked noisily at each finger with an exaggerated show of pleasure. Watching me impatiently, her eyes narrowed in jealous scorn.

"I want you girls to be on your very best behavior tonight. Our company is Father Poole, one of Jackie's, I mean Jack's teachers."

My fifteen-year-old brother, Clarence Jackson, later known as C.J., was named after our Father, Clarence Joseph. Ever since starting Jesuit High School, he had insisted on being called Jack instead of Jackie.

"Father Poole has been in Oregon for only a few months," Mom continued. "Your dad and I thought it would be nice to make him feel welcome. He's been teaching in a Mission School in Alaska for several years and has a lot of interesting stories and pictures he'd like to share with us.

"Your dad will be home in a little over an hour, so you girls finish up your snack and go up to your rooms. I want you to do your homework before dinner tonight."

Roseanne and I exchanged a suspicious and conspiratorial glance. It had been a long time since I could remember Mom being in such a good mood. Though it was really nice seeing her so cheerful—and, lucky for us, enthusiastically cooking what promised to be a delicious dinner—it was also confusing.

Rosie, Jack, and I had gotten pretty used to Dad's cooking in recent days, most of which invariably came out of a can or from a box out of the freezer. Mom had been gone a lot over the past year, on one or another of what she referred to as "retreats" or "extended vacations." These retreats, usually over a three-day weekend, were held at the Our Lady of Peace Retreat Center, just a few miles from our home, run by the Sisters of St. Mary's.

"The extended vacations" were at Morningside, a home in Portland run by the Jesuit Society of Oregon, where Mom would stay a few weeks, on one occasion for three months. We went to visit her there a few times. It was like a nice apartment complex in a pretty park-like setting, with lots of trees and flowers and an outdoor grotto with statues of various saints. At the time, I couldn't fully grasp why Mom went on these so-called vacations without the rest of the family. All too soon I would learn the unwelcome truth.

But tonight promised to be like old times, before Mom started having what Roseanne and I called sad spells and needed to go on retreats and vacations. Before the days when she would spend hours listening to melancholy, old-timey music on the record player, oftentimes singing along, with tears running down her face. Sometimes she would play these same sad songs on the piano or the guitar.

It was during these despondent moods that she would tell Roseanne and me stories of when she was a little girl, of how she had felt unwanted and neglected growing up in such a large family during the Great Depression. Countless times she told us how much she longed to hear her father say "I love you."

"I waited my whole life to hear those three little words, but they never came." She'd stare past us, as though seeing into her sad childhood. "And my mother, God rest her soul, she was always so gloomy. I believe her depression started when my oldest brother, Frank, died. It was on a Sunday when he drowned. She believed it was God's punishment on her for having missed Mass that day."

Her sister Elsie had said that something also died in their mom when Frank passed. "It was like a light went out in her heart, and she forgot how to laugh."

"Frank was her firstborn, her shining star," Mom had said. "I was the tenth born of her fourteen children, and by the time I was born, Mom's depression was so bad that my older sisters pretty much had to raise me. I was a tagalong wherever they went, and I can tell you they resented me for that."

When Mom had these sad spells, one story invariably led to another.

"I was six when the family planned a picnic. I ran back into the house to get my doll just before it was time to leave. When I got back, they'd left. No one even noticed I was missing. I sat alone in the yard and cried and cried all day long."

I tried to imagine what it must have felt like to be forgotten and not missed. It made me so sad to think of it. Even though Mom went away a lot, I knew she missed me. I really missed her when she was gone, but she always came home. Though I found it confusing, I just knew she would never go away and forget me... would she?

Another especially painful experience she told us about (though not in great detail) was how an older male family member had sexually abused her when she was a young teenager. And as if this wasn't bad enough, when she tried to tell her mother about it, she accused Mom of lying. Her mother admonished her that God would surely punish her for telling such awful stories about her own family and warned her that if she told her father, he would probably whip her. Consequently, the abuse continued, and she was forced to hide this painful secret with no one to protect her.

I felt bad for her—that she didn't feel loved, wanted, or protected by her parents. I think because of that, she tried extra hard to show us how much she loved us.

She was extremely protective of us, especially around strange men, even family friends. And no doubt because of Frank's drowning accident, whenever we were near a body of water, she would sit on the shore watching us like a hawk. But I think that all of this was a huge effort for her on top of being so sad all the time.

One thing that especially bewildered me was that her sad spells only seemed to get worse over time, not better. Oh, she might be in a good mood for a short time after she'd come home from one of her "vacation/retreats," like she missed us, but it wasn't long before she'd be right back to playing her sad songs and staring out the window.

We had moved into our brand-new house in the fall of 1963, and at first this seemed to make her really happy. And it was fun going shopping downtown with Mom and Dad for new furniture at The Maple Shoppe. And so exciting when it was all delivered in a big truck.

For a couple years, life was exciting: the planning, moving, and shopping—everything shiny and new. My parents even hired a professional landscaper, and in the spring and summer we all pitched in to help plant what seemed a bazillion trees and bushes.

In my young mind, Mom seemed happy for a while, but I reasoned she got bored when the newness wore off, and then she had all this shiny stuff she had to keep clean and that big yard full of plants and grass to take care of. So I guessed that's when she needed those retreat/vacations—to get some rest from all that cleaning and yard work.

What I came to realize later was that she was trying to fill a big hole in her heart with things that not only didn't fit but eventually left a greater feeling of emptiness.

✂ ✂ ✂

I was just finishing up the last of my homework assignment when the doorbell rang. Struggling out of my school uniform, I frowned at the dress and lacy socks Mom had laid out on my bed. I would have much preferred my usual comfy jeans, T-shirt, and tennis shoes.

"This feels pretty stupid to be getting so dressed up on a Wednesday."

Roseanne entered my room with dramatic flair, spinning in a tight circle, the pleats of her skirt twirling in a rainbow of color.

"Yeah. You'd think we were going to be meeting the Pope or something."

"Shut the door, Cinderella!" I chucked my balled-up jumper at her head. "I'm not done getting dressed." My jumper hit the wall with a dull thud when she ducked. "Mom warned us to be on our best behavior," I reminded Roseanne as I pulled my dress over my head.

Though less than enthusiastic about having to dress up on a Wednesday, I was undeniably curious about the evening's company. We had never had a priest come to our house before, let alone come for dinner.

After I finished dressing, Rosie and I tiptoed to the top of the stairs. From this vantage point we could peek around the corner and see into the dining room. I held a forefinger to my lips, and with a hushed *pssst* I motioned for Rosie to sit down. We sat on the top step, giggling nervously under our breath, intent on a few minutes of covert observation.

As we watched Mom busy herself with serving her guest a cup of coffee, her obvious delight in his presence was evident. He sat with his back to us, paying her his undivided attention. I remember thinking how pretty she looked when she smiled. How nice it was to hear her laugh. Her eyes sparkled when he let out a hearty chuckle in response, apparently enjoying their private joke.

My mother was a beautiful woman, and I felt a warm sense of pride and pleasure at seeing her dressed in one of her favorite outfits. I sighed as I watched her, thinking that the shimmery blue color of her dress made her cheeks look especially rosy. She must have gone to the beauty shop, for her hair was shiny and wavy, with pretty reddish highlights. I noticed too that she had taken the time to put on lipstick, and bit of rouge accentuated her lovely rosy high cheek bones. And I was pleased to see that she was wearing her pearl earrings and necklace set Dad had given her as an anniversary gift.

I found it impossible to suppress my delight. Mom must have heard our giggles, for she looked up and shook her head, a chagrined smile lifting her lips.

The man in the chair stood, turned, and looked up at us. A friendly smile spread across his handsome face.

Mom smiled up at us in obvious delight. "Come on down here, you two, and come meet our dinner guest."

As we entered the dining room, Roseanne walked shyly behind me, poking me in the back, prodding me forward. It seemed so strange to see a priest in his black uniform and white collar, standing in our dining room. At St. Mary's I was used to seeing nuns in their habits, the long black dresses with the head coverings, and sometimes a priest would walk down the hall when he wasn't in the chapel.

Although I was accustomed to seeing our parish priest, Father Gerace, when we went to St. Cecilia's for Mass, I had seen him in more casual settings, like at the annual Spaghetti Dinner held in the parish social hall. But it felt very strange having one in our house, especially because he didn't look like any priest I had ever seen. They were all old, stodgy, and serious, except for the one time I saw Father Gerace at a spaghetti dinner behaving very silly. (Dad joked later about how Father Gerace had been drinking the sacramental wine with his spaghetti.) This priest was much younger and handsome, with glossy black hair and eyes that sparkled when he smiled.

"So nice to finally meet you." He bent his knees, and with his hands on his thighs, brought himself to my eye level. "You must be Mary." He extended a thumb and forefinger to my chin, gently tipping my head back just a bit. He winked up at Mom. "You're right, Martha, she does have beautiful brown eyes."

Then he peeked around my shoulder. "And you must be Roseanne. What a beautiful dress. I am honored to meet such a lovely princess."

I stepped aside, nudging Rosie toward him. She demurred, tucking her chin against her shoulder and darting her eyes at the floor, at Mom, and then briefly up at him before looking back at the floor with great intent.

Mom stood behind our guest, smiling with obvious pride at both of her little darlings.

"Girls, this is Father Poole. Now what do you say when you are introduced?"

We chimed right on cue. "Nice to meet you, Father Poole."

"And so polite. My goodness, Martha, you have quite the young ladies here."

Father Poole straightened and reached to the dining table for a small envelope. "I brought you both a little something." He reached into the envelope and presented us each with a Holy Card.

Accepting these dutifully, I looked up at Mom, seeking some further direction.

Before she had the chance to instruct us, however, the priest went on. "And I also have a little something else." He reached into the pockets of his trousers and extended both closed fists toward us. "Mary." He waggled one fist, encouraging me to reach out for the procured gift.

I looked up at Mom, and when she nodded her approval, I presented a palm up in anticipation of his gift.

"Your Mother tells me you are quite the horsewoman."

I noted acutely his use of words, in lieu of the usual *horse-crazy girl*. Into the palm of my now sweaty palm, he placed a small statue of a glistening black horse, legs extended in a full gallop.

Mom raised her eyebrows. "What do you say, Mary?"

"Thank you, Father Poole."

And then to Roseanne he extended his other closed fist, to which she eagerly reached out her waiting palm.

He opened his fist. "And I hear that you are a big cat lover." A small figurine of a longhaired white kitten wrapped around a ball of bright blue yarn dropped into her waiting hand. "I'm a bit of a cat lover myself. Unfortunately, we are not allowed to have any at the rectory here because one of the brothers is allergic. But we had several cats at the mission in Alaska.

Roseanne looked directly at him now, her shyness waning as she accepted his gift with a firm, "Thank you, Father Poole."

"You girls go on up to your rooms and put your gifts away," Mom directed us. "Then wash your hands and come back down and set the table. Your father and Jack will be home shortly, and then we'll have supper."

Roseanne and I raced upstairs to put away our newly acquired treasures. There was a charged air of excitement around this man's presence in our home, and my mother's delight was evident and, at least on my part, contagious.

❃   ❃   ❃

Returning to the dining room, Roseanne and I set the table as our mother led her guest into the living room to finish his coffee.

In spite of, or perhaps because of her own lack of what she referred to as a proper upbringing, our mother deemed it vital that each of her children understand the fundamentals of manners, etiquette, and social grace. Setting a "proper" table was just one element of this early training.

By her own self-determination to rise above the backward ways of the poverty and neglect she was raised in, she schooled each of us in all the refinements and graces one could hope for in a middle-class, Catholic family in 1964. Though we resisted grievously, as any child would, to this day I am grateful (and, I confess, sometimes smugly proud) that I know how to set a proper table, answer a phone politely, address my elders with respect, remember always to say please and thank you, introduce my guests with decorum, and am conscientious about sending thank-you notes.

As much as it was important to her that she prepare us for a better future, I have no doubt that the image of The Lovely Family was very important to her self-worth. Her sense of accomplishment as a wife and mother were just one of the tenuous threads of value holding her together at that time.

As we continued to set the table for this very special dinner, I addressed Roseanne with an air of superiority. "Not like that. Put the knife on the inside." Rearranging the faulty setting with smug authority, I parroted our mother, acting out each instruction in turn.

"Both forks to the left of the plate, dinner fork inside, salad fork to the outside." I demonstrated. "Now put the table knife and spoon to the right of each plate; knife to the inside, spoon to the outside."

Roseanne huffed. "I know, I know."

"And don't forget to fold the napkin like this." I illustrated with artistic presentation. "And place it like that under the knife. Put the spoon to the right of the plate, you dummy!" With disgust I grabbed at the spoon she was putting in the wrong place, but she refused to let it go.

"Place a water glass to the right of each plate"— I tugged on the spoon—"precisely at two o'clock," I ordered.

Just then Roseanne let go of the spoon. It flipped out of my hand, flew through the air, and hit the sliding glass door. It dropped to the floor in a noisy clatter.

"Is everything all right in there?" Mom called from the living room.

I scurried to retrieve the errant spoon. Roseanne and I held our breath, anticipating chastisement, but, lucky for us, as if on cue and distracting her attention from our misbehavior, our father's car pulled into the driveway, its headlights cutting a bright path into the front room.

"Oh, good, here's Clarence and Jack." Mom sighed, clearly pleased that her little dinner party was moving along just as she had planned.

"Daddy, Daddy," my sister and I cried out as we ran to meet him coming through the front door. Rosie grabbed him around one leg, and I hugged around his waist as we took our positions, each standing on top of one of his work boots.

"Now, girls, settle down," Mom said as Dad monster-walked down the short entryway, with his two squealing and giggling appendages.

Father Poole extended his hand. "Hello, Clarence."

"Hello to you too." Dad shook his hand heartily as our mother escorted Roseanne and me to the sofa, where we sat squirming impatiently under the frowning scrutiny of her disapproving eye.

As Dad and Father Poole chatted amiably, Jack entered the house and more greetings and polite banter followed until Dad announced his need to clean up a bit before dinner.

"Something smells great." He winked at Mom. "I'll be right back. Make sure and save me some."

Over the course of dinner, Father Poole talked about his life on the mission field in Alaska, speaking passionately of his love for the native people and of the awesome beauty of the land. After dinner we all gathered in the living room for a slide show presentation. The images of the people with smiling faces and in native dress, the strangeness of the wildlife, and the vastness of the barren wilderness and mountainous landscapes captivated me.

As much as I was spellbound by the beautiful slides and the stories of this amazing place, I believe each of us sitting at the table that night were enchanted by Jim Poole, the "winsome and sincere man of God."

Over the duration of the school year, he was a regular guest. It became a common sight to see him relaxing in our living room on a Saturday afternoon, wearing one of our father's shirts. (My mother would give him these to wear during his visits, so he could be more comfortable by not having to wear his starched collar and jacket.) It was not unusual to see his car in the driveway when we came home from school. Most often he would be sitting at the table drinking coffee with Mom, deep in serious conversation, which often ended abruptly whenever one of us kids entered the room.

Frequently he would babysit Roseanne and me after school when our mother had one of her many doctors' appointments. I especially enjoyed when he sat with us because he told us lots of interesting stories and sometimes taught us card tricks. Often he brought little gifts—usually they were religious items, like Holy Cards, but occasionally he brought a special treat, like candy or a soft drink. Though we all enjoyed his company, none of us seemed to delight in his visits as much as Mom did. I was grateful to see my mother smiling and happy once again, especially when Father Poole came to visit. It appeared that she was finally getting better.

My relief at that time was only slightly shaded by an increasing tension I observed between my parents. I sensed it in my mother's covert looks of annoyance and disdain at my father—how she would roll her eyes in exasperation at any of my father's comments that held even the slightest bit of criticism. I winced inwardly as I noted my father's frustration, his ineffective attempts to appease her.

When Dad objected to our guest's increasingly frequent visits, Mom began meeting with Father Poole for personal counseling in his office at Jesuit High. "He is the first person I've ever counseled with that truly understands me," she said.

During this same school year, we had another priest who frequently visited in our home: Father Frank Duffy, also a teacher at Jesuit High School. He was of a totally different temperament and personality from Father Poole. Father Duffy was quiet and serious, though by no means dour or unfriendly, just more priestly or fatherly. In his mid-fifties, which at this time seemed ancient to me, he had graying hair and thick bushy eyebrows.

"He's like a big brother to me," our mother said. He too became her friend and confidant. He would also occasionally babysit with Roseanne and me. And though I liked him well enough, he did not possess the engaging charm of the younger priest, Jim Poole, nor was he what you would think of as particularly handsome.

But none of that really mattered much to me at that time. All I cared about was that Mom was getting better, happy again, and if these priests were helping her, well then that was great! What I didn't feel so great about was the increasing tension I felt between my parents.

My parents did not fight openly (except for one terrible night, shortly before Father Poole was transferred back to Alaska). Mostly they would just not talk, or, when they did, they would speak in clipped, forced, polite tones and sigh a lot. I think of that period of time now as their Cold War. And indeed the air in our home felt frigid at times.

Often at night Roseanne and I would lay awake in bed listening to their muffled, angry voices that carried through the heat ducts. Sometimes we would get out of bed and sit together on the floor, with our ears pressed to the heat register in our bedroom, trying to hear what they were saying. Occasionally we would hear Father Poole's name mentioned in these heated discussions, and always my mother would defend him as "someone who was finally helping me with my problems."

As I mentioned earlier, during the previous few years, Mom had been going on retreats, vacations, and—oh, did I mention that she saw lots of doctors? At the time I didn't really understand what kind of doctors they were but only that they were special doctors, not the usual kind you would go to if you needed a broken bone or a bad cut fixed. I knew she had been to a doctor and had been in a hospital a few years earlier for what she called female problems, and, because of the operation she had, she would not be able to have any more babies. Well, that was fine with me, I reasoned, because she already had six kids, and my oldest sister, Diana, even had a baby.

But she told me these doctors were supposed to help her with her nerves and with her sad spells. I know they gave her some very strong medicine, and my dad wasn't too happy about it. I heard him telling my sister Diana one day, "Your mom takes one pill to help her wake up in the morning and another to get to sleep at night." Then he laughed. "Yep, she's got her puppy uppers and her doggy downers." He also referred to one of her pills as Mother's little helpers.

I thought this was pretty funny. But it was all very confusing to me at the time. I just knew I wanted her to be like she used to be—my normal happy mom—instead of always moping around, all sad and grouchy. So I was glad she had Father Poole and Father Duffy to help her.

But then in June 1965, at the end of that school year, Father Poole came by the house to say good-bye. He was going back to his beloved Alaska, this time to a town called Barrow. The Church had another mission for him, and he seemed very happy to be going back there. But our mother was sad, and I could tell she was trying very hard not to cry when she, Rosie, and I stood in the driveway, watching him drive away.

Chapter Three
CLARENCE

September 1967

The dining room table came from The Maple Shoppe, a local business specializing in home furnishings. It was part of a set, with leaves and chairs enough to comfortably accommodate twelve people. The matching china hutch at the far end of the spacious dining room prominently displayed the remnants of a once extensive collection of delicate teacups and teapots, as well as a variety of hand-painted plates and small china figurines.

In the adjacent formal living room, a large Early American–style sofa flanked by two matching easy chairs were each tastefully embellished with maple trim. The remaining pieces, which included two end tables with matching lamps and a large coffee table, were also made of or trimmed with this same wood. Every room in the house had been lovingly designed and decorated when it was finished just four years prior.

Clarence Mueller sat at the dining room table, his left hand cradling his favorite mug, and although stained and chipped, it had a good solid feel in his hands. It was filled with a bitter black mixture of instant coffee he so often enjoyed and jokingly referred to as a good ol' cup a' mule sweat. In his right hand he balanced a pen between his index and middle finger, which he tap, tap, tapped on the blank page of a ledger. Preparing to enter the current month's bills, he sat for several moments staring absently into the space before him.

Gulping a big swallow of the now lukewarm coffee, he realized the futility of even attempting to make the numbers balance. A rising sense of anxiety rose up from his belly to his chest and his pen tap-tapped faster and faster—the overwhelming magnitude of his current situation staring back at him from the page of the ledger.

Setting down his mug, he thumbed through the stack of unpaid bills. He tossed the pen onto the table and massaged the tension from his neck, and then he reached into his pocket for a cigarette. That always seemed to calm him in moments like this.

"Hey, girls, how's dinner comin' along?" he called out to his two young daughters in the kitchen before taking a deep drag from his cigarette.

It was their task tonight to put together some kind of a meal from the pantry of canned goods he tried to always keep in stock.

"Zee sheff is almost redee," mimicked nine-year-old Roseanne in her best imitation of a current television advertisement for a popular brand of canned foods. "Tonight's dinnah is ravioli and frensch cut green beans."

"Dinnah is served," hollered twelve-year-old Mary from the back of the kitchen. She tossed the can opener into a drawer then pulled a stack of plates from the cupboard above. Walking past the open drawer she slammed it shut with a swing of her hip.

Pushing aside the stack of bills and closing the ledger, Clarence turned to watch as Mary set the table and Roseanne scooped the heated raviolis from the saucepan.

The dinner menu didn't vary much these days. It consisted of whatever was quick, easy, relatively inexpensive, and, hopefully, nutritious. Lord knows he was doing his best, but cooking and meal planning had never been his area of expertise. With Martha away, he was learning to do a lot of things he had never expected, as were the girls.

When the three were seated, Clarence led them in the familiar blessing over their meal. "Bless us, O Lord, and these, Thy gifts, which we are about to receive, from Thy bounty through Christ, our Lord."

"Amen," the three voices chimed in unison.

This was one of the many traditional Catholic prayers he had learned over the years. Martha had been raised in a strict old-school Catholic home, and he had agreed to convert to the faith as part of their pre-marriage arrangement. Though not an openly religious man, he had remained faithful to the tenets of the faith.

Looking across the table at his two youngest daughters, he watched as they devoured their meal. A mixture of love, pride, and distress filled him. He was concerned over their poor table manners, yet he grew weary of reminding them. He thought of how much they were missing without their mother's presence and example.

He felt a surge of pride as he admired the natural beauty of their still innocent preadolescence. Roseanne with her impish turned-up nose and the way her eyes danced when she smiled, and Mary's dark eyes and hair, so like his own.

These two were the youngest of his six children. The three older girls had already moved away and had busy lives of their own. His only son, Clarence Jr., whom everyone knew as Jack, was a seventeen-year-old high school senior. Having recently started an after-school job flipping burgers at McDonald's, they were seeing less and less of him around the house, especially at dinnertime.

"You two had better slow down."

The admonished girls continued to inhale their meal. He was becoming especially concerned about Mary's eating habits. He had discovered her sneaking into the refrigerator and cupboards for snacks, and he had noticed the little rolls forming around her middle and her cheeks getting rounder.

He had never concerned himself about these things before, as he had considered such subject matter no-man's-land, a mother's role. How could a married man with five daughters still find women such a mystery?

He didn't want to scold Mary too harshly, knowing this was a sensitive subject. He'd learned that much about females. Best to tread carefully in this area.

In the past, Martha had always been so conscientious about her personal appearance. It seemed she had forever been on a diet and had always taken the time to look nice—clean, slim, and well-groomed. She was still a very beautiful woman, though in the past two years she had gained a considerable amount of weight. Yet even after twenty-six years of marriage, she could still cause his heart to skip a beat when they dressed up to go out dancing.

Oh, how they danced! Ballroom, swing, and, their all-time favorite, square dancing! They had been members of an active square dance club that hosted regular gatherings, competitions, and social events all over the Northwest.

He sighed. That all seemed so long ago. These days his greatest form of recreation was bowling. Tuesday and Friday nights were big league nights. Most Tuesdays he took the girls along, sitting them down with Cokes and French fries. They seemed to enjoy hanging out with the other kids who tagged along with their parents.

On Fridays the girls stayed overnight with friends or cousins, or they went roller skating or to a movie. Occasionally, they'd stay home, in which case the TV would babysit. He felt a little guilty about that and worried what they might be up to when he was gone, but he just wasn't willing to give up his nights out. They were a welcome distraction after working hard all day, hammering out dents on cars at the body shop, welding and repairing damage. He had worked for the same shop for almost twenty-five years.

Examining a bruise starting to form under his left thumb, where his hammer had missed its intended target earlier in the day, he knew he would probably lose the nail. It sure wouldn't be the first time, and probably not the last time either.

He scratched at the calluses on the palms of his hands. They reminded him of worn leather gloves. Clarence smiled. They may not be much to look at, but he was grateful for the many skills learned over the years that required the use of these old paws.

He could build or fix just about anything mechanical. He was adept at plumbing, wiring, and a multitude of other skilled labor jobs. He considered himself an artist really, able to build a house from the ground up. He would regularly transform a seemingly hopeless mess of a wrecked car into a vehicle that looked as good as new, sometimes better than new. Though he prided himself in that, he lamented that he couldn't work the same "magic" in his personal life.

After the evening meal, Clarence sent the girls upstairs to their bedrooms where they were currently working on their school homework... at least that was what they were supposed to be doing. He thought of going up to check in on them—right after he finished cleaning up the kitchen.

He wiped down the counters and the stovetop then set the teakettle back on for his after-dinner coffee. As he waited for the water to heat, he glanced around the kitchen for any more areas of damage control, that is, clean-up from the meal preparation.

He knew that the girls were trying, but they paid as much attention to detail as you could expect from most unattended nine- and twelve-year-olds.

I'm sure I could use some work in this area as well. He chuckled, noting the layer of greasy film on the glass doors of the display cabinet above the breakfast bar.

The cabinet was once home to a complete twelve-place setting of fine china, along with crystal plates and goblets and a variety of bowls and serving platters. The few remaining goblets, plates, and assorted pieces of china were now scattered in disarray in the cabinet and covered in a thin layer of dust. A small crystal dish held a variety of coins, an agate, along with nuts, bolts, and washers. At one end of the cabinet was a stack of grocery coupons, receipts, and scraps of paper containing phone numbers and messages.

As Clarence absently sorted through the pile of papers, the teakettle whistled. He poured the boiling water into his mug, and, stirring his coffee, he returned to the dining table to the stack of bills still awaiting his attention.

He opened the ledger and entered the date at the top of the first blank page: *September 1967.* At least he was confident of that much. At this moment there wasn't a whole lot else he could be certain about.

Just a few short years ago they had been living the American Dream. How did they get to this place anyway? And how could he get the family out of this mess? The unwelcome but all too familiar sense of panic gripped him.

He ran his fingers through his hair, still jet-black, even at forty-seven, then arched back in his chair to relieve the knot forming at the base of his spine. Drawing a cigarette from the open pack on the table, he let out a deep sigh and began entering figures.

Closing the desk drawer on his monthly task, the sound of the television in the living room brought him back to the present. This was one of his favorite evenings at home, and the girls had already tuned in to one of their regular programs: *The Carol Burnett Show.*

Now there was good, old-fashioned, clean fun.

Opening the refrigerator, he reached for a cold beer. He rationed himself to two, three at the most—just enough to take that raw edge off and help him relax for the evening. Only on the rarest of weekend evenings did a full six-pack "do the job."

On those occasions he liked to form the cans into a pyramid in front of the fireplace—three on the bottom, then two, and with the last strategically placed on top, he'd feel nicely relaxed.

After an especially hard week, on the rarest of rare of times, he'd arrange the six-pack of cans in bowling-pin fashion, which required a seventh beer to use as the bowling ball. And as the "ball" made contact with the "pins," he would shout, "Strike!" then climb the stairs to his bedroom.

Pulling a couple of pillows from the sofa where Mary and Roseanne lay stretched out at opposite ends, he tossed them in front of the unlit fireplace hearth, preparing to settle in for the remainder of the evening.

"You guys done with your homework?" he asked, scrunching and wiggling into the foam of the pillows. Adjusting them, he finally found the perfect arrangement and allowed himself to fully sink into his cozy nest. Receiving no response, he repeated his inquiry in the direction of the sofa, where the girls appeared to be engrossed in the program.

Roseanne chuckled at the hilarity of the program's antics, and Mary rolled her eyes and kicked her feet at her sister under the shared blanket.

"Jeez, your toenails are sharp. Get 'em off my legs." Mary recoiled then kicked Roseanne harder.

"Get your legs off my side of the couch," Roseanne said.

Had it not been for the distracting buffoonery of the program, a full-blown foot fight would have ensued.

Clarence's familiar belly laugh filled the room with a comfortable calm, and the three relaxed in their prospective orbits. Thoughts of homework, bills, and household chores were all but forgotten.

⌘ ⌘ ⌘

The house was silent at two AM. Only the hum of the refrigerator and the drone of the furnace turning on could be heard. Absent were the everyday noise and chaos that accompanied life with three young people, along with their many friends and activities. But in the quiet house, there was no one to interrupt him; no one clamoring for his attention, demanding decisions; no ever present line of folks lined up with their hands out for money that just wasn't stretching as far as their demands. Even so, Clarence's mind was anything but quiet.

So many doctor bills piling up, and the local hospital recently sent a notice threatening to send the bills to a collection agency. And then there was the ambulance fee for the early morning ride that took Martha to the emergency room in July.

I might as well get up, make a cup of coffee, and enjoy the peace and quiet. He pulled on a T-shirt over his pajama bottoms. *I won't be able to sleep anyway.*

He found his comfortable spot back at the dining room table and there he sat, like so many nights of late, the quiet house and his thoughts his only company.

So many thoughts, all a-tangle—some dark and sad, others hopeful and encouraging. Closing his eyes, he took a few deep breaths and attempted to still the many voices in his head.

Just relax. Things will work out just fine. They always do, somehow. And yet the internal chattering continued to plague him, even in the quiet sanctuary of his comfortable home in the middle of the night.

⚒ ⚒ ⚒

Hearing footsteps on the stairs, he looked up to see Mary shuffling into the room, squinting against the bright light of the crystal chandelier.

"Daddy, are you all right?" Rubbing the sleep from her eyes, Mary tugged at the belt of her Snoopy bathrobe and dropped into a chair next to him. "I got up to go to the bathroom and saw the light on down here." Lowering her head onto his shoulder, she closed her eyes.

Exhaling, he stroked her long dark hair then gave the top of her head a little pat. "I'm okay, honey, just having a hard time sleeping tonight. Go on back to bed now and get your beauty sleep."

After a moment Mary pushed up from the chair and made her way slowly back up the stairs. At the top of the landing she looked down to see her father staring into his coffee cup, as though all the answers to his problems were at the bottom of that cup.

Chapter Four
SISTERS

Sacramento Airport, October 2006

Airports are a great place for people watching. With so many little dramas unfolding, waiting for flights can be interesting and a good way to pass the time. Roseanne's plane was due to arrive in about an hour, so I sat back and looked around at the people hurrying either to make their flights or to greet family and friends.

To my right, a young, slightly disheveled woman, with a look of exhaustion familiar to those who have traveled with young children, held in her arms a tiny whimpering baby. A small boy busily amused himself, weaving between her legs, bumping into nearby (greatly annoyed) passengers as they waited in line. The little darling was about to push this poor mother to the extreme limits of her patience with myriad questions and complaints, beginning with, "Mommy, when are we going to get there?" Quite obviously she had run out of energy to field his questions, let alone discipline him. As she stood in line, zombie-like, trying her best to ignore him, she gently rocked her infant, whose whimpering had evolved into full-blown screaming. I wondered where she was going and what her story could be.

I decided this felt like a good time to take a short walk while I waited for Roseanne to arrive. As I made my way toward the farther end of the airport, the wails of the infant were swallowed up by voices over the loud speaker alerting passengers to arriving and departing flights. I strolled past one gate and observed a young couple embracing with the passion of new love. They would soon board a plane destined for Kona, Hawaii—most likely on their honeymoon.

In the adjoining boarding gate, a group of military personnel milled about, and I could only imagine what God-forsaken places they were headed to or coming home from. What horrors would they soon be experiencing or had they seen?

I walked a big loop around the boarding/arrival gates, stopping to browse in a bookstore along the way; then I made my way back down the hallway toward Roseanne's arrival gate. I felt a great sense of gratitude that my time in California involved neither caring for small children (my two sons were both in their thirties) nor going off to war. And although I would not be going to Hawaii, I said a silent prayer of thanks for the wonderful lover waiting for me at home in Montana, my own version of paradise.

Shortly after I approached her gate, Roseanne stepped into the passenger arrival area. I watched as she peered intently among the mob of passengers, looking travel weary. When she spotted me, her face brightened and the fatigue visibly dropped from her. We embraced, and like little girls, jumped up and down, squealing with delight.

"Sister-Fest!" I sing-songed.

"Yeah, yeah, Sister-Fest!" Roseanne echoed. She rocked me while holding me by the shoulders at arm's length. We stood quietly for a few seconds, getting a good long look at each other before squealing all over again.

"All right then, let's get this show on the road," I said, with mock seriousness. Grasping the handle on my roller bag, I led the way to the rental car counter.

We'd been planning this trip for several months. I'd flown in from Missoula, Montana, and Roseanne from Portland, Oregon, and we were both eager to "Let the fun begin!" Our plan was to spend two days in Sacramento with our oldest sister, Diana. Then we would drive through the Redwood National Park, the Sonoma and Napa valleys, continuing on to the coast to spend three days with our next oldest sister, Joan.

In our family of six siblings, our ages span over sixteen years. Diana, Joan, and Beth, the three oldest girls are each two years apart. C.J., the only boy, is four years younger than Beth; and Roseanne and I, the two youngest girls, are four years apart. Due to our ages and shared life experiences, Roseanne and I are quite close, as are Joan and Diana. Though at the time of this trip, Roseanne was forty-eight and I was fifty-one, we both shared the frustration of feeling like dumb little sisters when we gathered together with our older siblings. This will probably never change, it is so deeply ingrained, and I'm sure very it's common in most families. But still we desire the recognition of being seen as intelligent, adult women. On this particular trip, Rosie and I were hoping that by sharing some time together as grown-up sisters, we might help bridge this generation gap.

Roseanne was working through a Master's program in Marriage and Family Therapy, and as part of her schooling she had to write a paper entitled "Family of Origin." So the timing of this trip seemed doubly great for her. Though Roseanne's research was scholastic as well as personal, my interest was purely personal.

We both felt that our older sisters held the key to unlocking many long-held family secrets. So much of my childhood is a mystery to me, with many missing pieces of the puzzle of my youth, especially concerning my mother. When I reflect back on the time starting in the mid-1960s, I have the sense of an emotional grenade being covertly thrown into our home and shattering my seemingly perfect family into fragmented pieces. Because Roseanne and I were was so young, much was kept from us. Consequently, we have filled in many of these blank spaces with guesses and imaginings drawn from rumors and whispered secrets, trying to make sense of the confusion and chaos that was our reality. No doubt we were too young to understand the complexities of our parents' problems at that time, but now we must certainly be grown up enough to know the truth. Perhaps my older sisters would reveal some of these missing pieces during our time together.

❈ ❈ ❈

The visit with Diana went quickly. We spent a lot of time just sitting around relaxing, though one afternoon the three of us took a long, leisurely walk along the American River. The pleasant weather was unlike the sweltering heat I've experienced when visiting in the summer months. October is a great time to be in Sacramento.

On our last evening as we sat in Diana's cozy living room, Roseanne brought up the subject of her "Family of Origin" paper. I could tell she was a bit anxious, so I shot her a reassuring glance.

"Can you look this over and give me your feedback?" Roseanne asked as she handed Diana the multiple-page document. "I had to just wing it on a lot of this because I wasn't exactly sure about some of the facts. If you can clarify any of the sketchy details, I would really appreciate it. So, that's my disclaimer." She clenched her hands and gave a small nervous laugh.

Roseanne and I sat across the room, each sipping a glass of wine as Diana began reading. Every so often Diana would chuckle, look up from the page, and shake her head. At one point she closed her eyes, frowning and sighing deeply. When she finished, she set the pages in her lap and looked Roseanne squarely in the eye.

"What family did you grow up in?" Shaking her head, she rolled her eyes as and held out her glass and motioned toward the open wine bottle on the coffee table.

"Like I said, I had to wing it on a lot of that, so help me out here, okay?" Roseanne said.

I knew how badly Roseanne longed for Diana's approval, and my heart went out to my little sister. She shifted nervously in her chair as I filled Diana's glass. "All right then, fill me in on what I'm missing or what I'm not remembering correctly." Reaching across the coffee table for the now empty bottle, Roseanne upturned it, shaking the last few drops into her glass. I jumped up and brought back a fresh bottle from the kitchen.

Over the next few hours of sharing our second bottle of wine, we discussed the contents of the paper in light of our differing perceptions and experiences growing up. As the afternoon spilled into evening, we all began to relax, enjoying our wine and one another's company. Roseanne and I asked Diana a lot of questions concerning our mother, with particular interest in hearing about Diana's relationship with her.

Diana told us that when she was in her early twenties, Mom had shared many confidences with her. "She wanted me to be an ally." She glanced from me to Roseanne. I saw a sadness in Diana I'd never seen before.

"She divulged a lot of very personal stuff. There were things she was deeply ashamed of and asked me to keep them to myself. It was a big responsibility to place on my shoulders at the time."

"Did she talk to you about her relationship with Father Poole?" I said.

"Yes, she did. She told me that they had had an affair and that she was still very much in love with him. I don't believe she ever forgave herself for what she no doubt thought of as her mortal sin. She was obsessed with the fantasy of their being in love. But she was tormented by the shame she felt over this and was devastated by what she perceived as his abandonment of her. Apparently she wrote him numerous letters over the years, but he never wrote back, never acknowledged their special relationship."

"You know, Diana, I always suspected that's what happened," I said. "Dad talked to me about that just shortly before he died. I was visiting one day, and he started to talk to me about Mom. He didn't go into great depth, and we didn't stay on the subject long, but he did tell me that Mom was in love with Father Poole. It was obviously a very sensitive and painful subject for him, even after so many years."

So there it was. The elephant in the room that no one ever wanted to acknowledge openly, the one big event that I always suspected was responsible for my mother's final undoing. Without a doubt, the tenuous threads of sanity that held her together at that time most certainly began to unravel irreparably the day Father Poole drove away from our home in June 1965. And as obsession and guilt over this lost love wrapped their tentacles around her mind, I believe she became blinded from seeing the goodness of her own soul.

Roseanne poured the last of the wine into her glass then handed Diana another piece of paper. "Maybe this will help shed some light on what really happened with Mom, or, rather, what happened *to* her. Beth sent me these articles about a year ago. She discovered one on a back page of the *Bend Oregon Bulletin* and the other was in the *Oregonian.* I have included them in my "Family of Origin" paper because I believe it is pertinent to our family's history."

Diana took a generous swallow of her wine then with a deep breath began to read. As she read, her eyes opened wider and wider. She looked over the top of the page across the room at Roseanne and me, then back to the page again, the color draining from her face. "Oh my God! This is unbelievable!" She shook her head as though that would help her grasp what she was reading.

Chapter Five
BACK PAGE NEWS

Sex-abuse suits embroil Jesuits in Northwest
[Portland] Oregon
The Oregonian
Monday, November 14, 2005
Ashbell S. Green
Posted by kshaw at November 14, 2005 07:33 AM

In the long shadow of the archdiocese of Portland bankruptcy, an Oregon-based Jesuit province faces a growing priest-abuse litigation crisis of its own.

In the last few years, as many as 100 people have filed sex-abuse lawsuits accusing more than a dozen priests and volunteers of the Oregon Province of the Society of Jesus, according to plaintiff's attorneys….

…The bulk of the alleged abuse occurred in remote Alaskan Eskimo villages that during the long winters are almost completely cut off from the rest of the world.

"There's no one to tell, no one to turn to, no one to talk to," said Elsie Boudreau, an Anchorage woman who was sexually abused by a priest when she was a girl. Boudreau settled her case for $1 million in April.

The Rev. John D. Whitney, the Portland-based provincial superior, admitted that the Rev. James Poole had committed sexual abuse and apologized to Boudreau.

Several Northwest Jesuits facing sex-abuse lawsuits
The associated Press
Portland [Oregon]
The [Bend] Bulletin, Tuesday November 15, 2005

...Cooke said documents indicate that when the Portland-based Jesuits learned about sex-abuse allegations as far back as 1960, they moved the priest to another village or another state. Cooke said that in some cases, pedophile priests from another part of the country were sent to Alaska....

...Although the provinces' headquarters are in Portland, very little of the litigation directly touches Oregon....

...The most immediate legal issue on the horizon for the Jesuits is a trial scheduled for February in Nome, involving Poole, whom five people have accused of sexual abuse. The Jesuits and the Diocese of Fairbanks have settled two Poole cases, including the one with Boudreau. Poole lives in an assisted living facility in Spokane.[1]

❊ ❊ ❊

After Diana finished reading the newspaper article about Jim Poole, she studied Roseanne and me. Deep concern darkened her eyes. "So, were either of you molested by him?"

"No, I have no such memory," I said without hesitation.

Roseanne shook her head and almost yelled her response. "No!"

The lady doth protest too much, methinks.

Her discomfort with this question was quite obvious to me, and I'm sure it must have been to Diana as well, so much so that we didn't push the subject with her any further.

Roseanne emphasized that over the past year, since Beth had sent her the news clipping, that she had been thinking a lot about what had happened to Mom in relation to her involvement with Father Poole. "I'm giving serious thought to contacting this attorney." She tapped the article.

When Diana handed Roseanne her papers, she regarded us as though trying to scrutinize something in our faces.

"I'm not sure what will come out of it, but maybe it will help shed some light on what really happened to Mom," Roseanne said.

Diana shook her head, rose, and started clearing the coffee table of our evenings' libations.

"I don't know why you'd want to open that old can of worms, Rosie. I don't see how any good could ever come of it." She bid us good night, making it clear that she was done talking about this.

The first tremor of the imminent emotional earthquake came in the form of that newspaper article. On a back page, sandwiched between the Thanksgiving recipes and the local sports scoreboard, was the name of the man none of us cared ever to hear of again. Yet, little did we know the extent of the evil that this "Holy Man of God" had woven into the fabric of our family. The magnitude of it was soon to be revealed, activating a shock wave that spread its deep emotional fissures through each one of us, reaching nearly forty years into the past.

❊ ❊ ❊

October 2006, 8 AM, Hwy 101, en route from Sacramento to the California Coast.

Startling awake, I felt a sudden wave of nausea as Roseanne jerked the steering wheel, swerving recklessly into the far right lane. I'm not sure what was worse; the queasy stomach or the dull throbbing between my eyes.

Though it did help us to relax enough to discuss Mom, Father Poole, and the abuse cases, I was beginning to wonder if it had been such a great idea to open that second bottle of wine the previous night. I had tossed and turned until well past midnight, and this morning we were up and on the road by 7 AM.

I was certainly feeling the lack of sleep and the effects of too much wine. But more than that, I was still trying to wrap my mind around all that we had talked about.

"Let's stop and get some breakfast," I said. "Maybe that'll help my headache."

"Good idea." Roseanne slowed for the upcoming exit.

After the waitress brought our food, I got right to the point. "So, Rosie, talk to me about last night."

"Yeah, sure." She spread a melting pat of butter across her pancake. "Like, about what exactly?"

I studied her for a moment, watching as she stirred sugar into her tea and then raised it toward her lips.

"Well, like for starters, did Father Poole molest you?"

Her cup stopped midway to her lips. She slowly raised her eyes to meet mine; then she set the cup back on the table. She took several deep sighing breaths, staring past me. Puckering and straightening her lips, she cocked her head to one side, as though formulating the right words.

"Yes, he did." She answered barely above a whisper and quickly looked down into her tea. Her shoulders slumped. Slowly she looked up into my eyes then back into her cup, as though for comfort.

I felt a sudden sensation, as if a heavy weight were pressing onto my chest.

"Why'd you tell Diana no, and why the hell didn't you ever tell me? I thought we shared everything."

"Are you kidding?! I've spent my whole life trying to forget about it." Looking up at me she shook her head, as though trying to clear away the evil memories. "I was just so young; I had no way of processing what happened to me. After a while I think it felt like maybe I had only imagined it or something, which really made me feel like I must be sick or something. But deep down I knew it did really happen. I have always felt so ashamed, like somehow it was my fault and that I was bad."

"But maybe if you had told me, I could have protected you." Reaching across the table, I placed my hand firmly on top of hers and the weight lifted slightly from my chest.

"I am your big sister, you know." Struggling with my own hurt feelings, the irrational ache of what felt like a betrayal, I shook my head. "I can't believe you didn't trust me enough to tell me."

"You know the funny thing is that I thought you knew." Roseanne looked up. I squeezed her hand, noticing the tears forming in the corner of her eyes.

"Are you kidding? I would have ripped his eyes out!" I squeezed her hand harder and the constriction over my heart released a bit more.

Roseanne pulled her hand away and took a long slow sip of her tea. She shrugged. "I know it doesn't make sense to you, but that's how I've had it all mixed up in my head all these years. You know, when he left, the day he drove away from our house, in my seven-year-old mind he ceased to exist. You can't imagine how confusing it has been for me to wrap my mind around the fact that he is still alive and that he did continue to exist apart from my memory."

We sat in silence a few minutes, each of us picking at our breakfasts. Roseanne stabbed a bite of pancake and pointed it at me. "I'm also beginning to see that Mom was a victim too. You know, we've always had this shameful little secret in our family about her having an affair with him, but the more I've thought about it, the more I've come to realize that he also preyed on her, that he took advantage of her emotional instability. He exploited her neediness!" She waggled her pancake-laden fork for emphasis before shoving it into her mouth. She speared and chewed on the rest of her pancake as though it were an old enemy. We remained quiet through the remainder of the meal, busily digesting all we had discussed. My appetite now gone, I stared absently at my half-finished breakfast as I wondered, *Where will this new revelation take our family next?*

Chapter Six
EMAILS OF DARK TALES

From: Ken Roosa
To: Roseanne Miller
Sent: Thursday November 16, 2006
Subject: Father Poole

Roseanne, I want to thank you for your courage in contacting me. I have some understanding of how terribly difficult it is to think about these events, let alone share them with a stranger. Your testimony would be of real value to the other women [Alaskan Natives] who have reported Father Poole. He and the Church are denying their truth and re-victimizing them in the process. I would very much like to talk to you. Please contact me directly via email at this address or phone me.

Ken

From: Roseanne Miller
To: Ken Roosa
Sent: Friday, November 17, 2006
Re: Father Poole

Ken,

I appreciate your sensitivity and empathy. I have had lots of therapy, so it's not so hard for me to talk about my life as it used to be. It took a lot of years out of my life and happiness, but like I said before, the sexual abuse was traumatic enough in itself, but what really ruined my childhood and much of my adult life was what Father Poole and the Catholic Church did to my mother....

I don't know much about the details of what happened between Father Poole and my mom. She was experiencing a lot of disappointment in her life and was going through menopause at the same time. She sought counseling from the priests. I was only 5 or 6 when this was going on, so I wasn't privy to a lot of the details, but I do remember a big brue ha ha [sic] and my mother being very distraught, hearing that Father Poole was transferred to Nome. [Initially he was transferred to Barrow.] I knew my mom liked him, so I thought she was just sad about his leaving. I was sad too and cried when he came to our house for a last visit. It wasn't until I was older that I found out about his affair with my mom. And things started to make sense to me. I was very sorry to read that he went on to continue this abuse up in Alaska. If he had not been transferred, it probably would have turned out much worse for me....

I have three sisters who are much older than me, 16, 14, and 12 years [at that time], respectively. They know more about what happened with Father Poole and my mom than anyone, but it's hard to get them to talk about it....

I hope this can be of some help.

Roseanne

From: Ken Roosa
To: Roseanne Miller
Sent: Monday, November 20, 2006
Re: Father Duffy

[Roseanne]

I really do appreciate your thoughtful and insightful comments on the situation. I just received a call from a client in Anchorage who was molested by Poole many times, starting when she was 6 yrs old. In 1966. She was molested in Barrow, Alaska, the year after Poole left Beaverton. She was just calling to check on the status of her case, and when I mentioned that I had heard from a woman in Oregon, she was excited and happy that you were willing to help her by testifying in her case if needed....

I also learned of other lawsuits filed against Father Francis Duffy[1]....

I don't want you to feel pressured, I am aware of how voluminous the records can be. I have a client from Milwaukee, OR, who was hospitalized numerous times and has been in continuous therapy for more than 10 years. Now that's a lot of records![2]....

If you want to meet and talk, that too can be arranged. I am going to a conference in S.Ca in early December. I could stop off in Portland on my way back and meet with you.

[Ken]

❦ ❦ ❦

November 27, 2006

"Happy birthday to you. Happy birthday to you. You look like a monkey and you smell like one too. Hee Hee! Hey, give me a call when—"

I grabbed the phone. "Hey, Rosie!"

"Screening your calls, ey?" She laughed.

"Oh, hi, Rosie." I greeted, short of breath. "I was just coming in from outside when I heard your message."

"And, yes, I do screen my calls. You know I only talk to the very best people."

"Well, how honored I am to be included in your best list. So, hey, happy birthday. What are you doing to celebrate?"

"Well, for starters, I've been out stacking firewood." I laughed. "And after I get over the excitement of that, I'm gonna go feed the horses."

"Boy, you really know how to live it up. Do try not to have too much fun. Seriously, happy birthday, you old fart. And happy belated Thanksgiving, too."

"Thanks, Rosie. And don't you forget, I am your elder, so you'd better show some respect here."

Today was my fifty-second birthday, just three days after Thanksgiving. With Christmas now less than a month away, the slight chill in the air as I stacked wood was just the beginning of another long cold Montana winter. But that was just fine with me. Since moving here in the early '90s, I had grown to love the change of seasons.

After a bit more of our usual teasing and several minutes exchanging stories about our Thanksgiving holiday, Roseanne's tone shifted abruptly and she grew quiet.

"So, what else is up?" I knew her well enough that I sensed by her unspoken words that something was on her mind.

"Well, I really don't want to put a damper on your birthday, but I do have something I need to talk to you about."

"Okay," I hesitated, not certain that I wanted to know. "I'm all ears."

"Remember the newspaper article I shared with you when we went to California? The one about Father Poole?" Her voice had taken on a serious tone.

"Hmm, newspaper article? I think I have a vague recollection." My attempt at levity fell flat. "Of course I remember. What about it?"

"I finally got up the nerve to contact the attorney that was named in that article. And we've been corresponding."

"So, has that been a good thing?"

"Well, good and bad. The good part is that he seems like a really caring, concerned person. But the bad thing is that I'm pretty scared about what all is going to come up for me if I continue to pursue this. Anyway, I was wondering if I could send you copies of some of our emails back and forth and you could tell me what you think."

"Sure, Rosie, go ahead and forward them to me, and I'll give you my take."

We chatted a few more minutes, mostly about upcoming Christmas plans. She was planning to spend Christmas at the Oregon Coast with our brother and his family as well as our sister Joan, who would be there visiting from California. After we hung up I sat there for some time, thinking about our conversation. I couldn't help but wonder where this all was going to lead, for Rosie, for myself, for our whole family.

⚹ ⚹ ⚹

Over the next few weeks after our phone conversation, as I received a deluge of forwarded emails, an ominous sense of just how big this "thing" might be grew within me. Some of the emails I couldn't finish reading. One was a forty-seven-page brief from the case of a Jane Doe 2, who was one of Father Poole's Alaskan victims. The horror of what this woman went through and the mental anguish she suffered throughout her life as a result was just too much for me to take in.

It seemed important to Rosie that I read these, but I just couldn't. Eventually she did talk to our sister Beth, who convinced me to "Suck it up and get on board," that we needed to truly show Roseanne our support. When I finally did read the Jane Doe 2 email, I began to realize more fully the extent of the evil involved and how important it was that we sisters be in this battle together.

Beth, Roseanne, and I have grown very close over the course of our adult lives. Because of our shared Christian faith, we are at times teasingly referred to as the "God Sisters."

Over the course of the next few years, as we worked to unravel the mysteries of our family's past, we grew even closer, supporting one another through prayer and deep conversation. We covered a lot of miles on long walks along the Pacific Ocean's shore, neighborhood parks, and a few mountain trails. We have also experienced a few uproarious mealtimes replete with hilarious antics and accompanied by a bottle of fine wine.

Though Roseanne was the lead in this grand play, and the second and third of the God Sisters had joined the act, it soon became apparent that all six of the Mueller siblings had a supporting role and would soon be called on stage.

❊ ❊ ❊

December 2006

Roseanne, Beth, and I were talking more and more frequently about Roseanne's conversations with the attorneys involved in the NW Jesuit sex abuse cases. Roseanne was still uncertain as to how, or even if, she wanted to proceed. All Beth and I could do was pray, listen, and encourage Rosie to do what she felt was right.

But these conversations—just thinking about what had taken place—as Diana had put it, "opening up that old can of worms," gave me a deep, unsettling feeling of dread. And I began to wonder as Diana had asked, *What good could possibly come of it?*

❊ ❊ ❊

December 1, 2006, More Forwarded Emails from Roseanne

November 30, 2006
From: Roseanne Miller
To: Ken Roosa
Subject: What is Alaska's time difference?

Ken,

I haven't called either of those women yet [the two women in Alaska who were involved in a lawsuit claiming sexual abuse by Father Poole]. I'm working my way up to it, I guess. Not knowing the time difference has been my excuse for the last couple days. Maybe I'll think up another one yet.

Yesterday I was starting a fire in the woodstove and was watching the wood sizzle as the fire squeezed out the wood's moisture at the cut end of the log, at the wounded end. The moisture dripped slowly like tears as the log reluctantly relinquished its lifeblood.

I have kept all this stuff about fathers Poole and Duffy very tightly tucked away into the do-not-go-there zone as if my life depended on it. I think I'm finally ready to admit that my life doesn't depend on it anymore. I realize that it may be time to let it go. But I can't guarantee that it won't have to be squeezed out.

[Another] reason I have held on to this is that if I talk about it in detail, it will make it real. I have never had to make it real before. I have had too much other trauma to deal with, so I just couldn't risk bringing this to life. I have had to prioritize. This is a coping mechanism you are probably well aware of. So I have been able to stay emotionally detached from the issue, and I would like to believe that I can stay emotionally detached even if I have to talk about it. I will try to the best of my ability, but I know I'm fooling myself.

However, I am pretty good at it, so don't be shocked if I can tell this story and seem emotionally unaffected. Even when I am devastated on the inside, I can hold it together on the outside pretty good. I've had forty-some years of experience doing it.

After my mother fell apart (shortly after Father Poole left for Alaska), she attempted suicide [numerous] times over the course of the next six years. My sister Mary and I experienced the fallout from this chaos but still had to go to school every day and pretend everything was okay.

Roseanne

⌘ ⌘ ⌘

I sat for the longest time staring at that last email, my heart aching for Roseanne. What she had been through all those years, keeping this horrible secret. And again I felt that familiar pang of guilt. Why didn't I know? Why didn't I protect her? The accusing voice taunted me for the hundredth time.

I took a deep breath and, with a long slow exhale, consciously reminded myself, *Let it go, Mary. Give it to God.* I stood and poured myself a second cup of coffee.

Cradling the warm mug, I glanced absently out the front window, the last few lines of her email still floating around in my head. "Mary and I experienced the fallout from this chaos but still had to go to school every day and pretend everything was okay."

Just then I remembered riding the school bus one morning right after Mom had been readmitted to the state hospital, following a short home visit. Someone on the bus shouted, "Hey, Mary, I hear your mom is back in the funny farm."

The mocking humor not only embarrassed me but also filled me with such humiliating shame that I felt physically ill.

"Yep, she's a real nut case." I laughed along with my fellow bus mates, the shell around my heart hardening a bit and filling me with an even greater sense of shame that I had not even tried to defend my own mother!

As the bus had pulled into the school parking lot, bile had risen into my throat. Rushing off the bus, I had hurried to the bathroom.

Roseanne mentioned at one point that fall that this attorney, Ken Roosa, wanted to talk to me and was wondering if I was interested in filing a claim as well. At that time Roseanne and I had a conversation about whether or not I too had been abused by either of these priests.

That was a difficult period of time for me, as I truly had no conscious, clear recollection of any childhood sexual abuse. I examined myself thoroughly, spending considerable time in prayer, seeking revelation if indeed this had happened. Perhaps I had buried it deep in my subconscious.

At one point Rosie said, "I just assumed that it had happened to you too, and that, like me, you just couldn't talk about it."

I assured her that I had no recall of any memories of abuse. Even so, I still felt a strange and frustrating sense of disorientation. I was really struggling with my lack of clear memories of that time.

There was so much chaos, confusion, and tight-lipped secrecy in our family during the time these priests were involved with our family. Along with the upheaval and disorder brewing all around us—my mother's emotional instability at the center—were the elements of the perfect storm that would ultimately shipwreck our entire family for many long pain-filled years.

Part Two

Chapter Seven
THE TERRIBLE NIGHT

Throughout the 1964–65 school year, when Jim Poole was teaching my brother at Jesuit High School, he was also counseling Mom and, on occasion, babysitting Roseanne and me. Mom was becoming increasingly dependent on his counsel and sought his help and support in a family crisis involving our sister Beth.

Beth had moved away from home in the summer of 1964 following her high school graduation. In February of 1965 she learned that she was pregnant, and she subsequently moved back home. In late March Mom took her along on one of her counseling session in which Mom and Father Poole made arrangements, per his counsel, to send Beth to a Catholic Charities home for unwed mothers in Spokane, Washington.

Beth felt that she had no recourse and reluctantly went along with their plan. In late May she was taken to the home where she remained until September, when her daughter was born and adopted by a young Catholic couple. Shortly after this heartbreaking experience, she returned home.

Nothing was ever mentioned or discussed openly, certainly not with Roseanne or me, before she left, during her absence, or upon her return. We were just told that she had gone to a special school, which didn't seem at all strange to me, since she had graduated from high school the year before and had already been out on her own for a while. It seemed only logical that she'd be attending a course of higher education.

Thus, Beth's secret stayed locked within the walls of her heart and mind, shrouded in guilt, shame, and deep regret for many years. This was just one of a number of family secrets closeted away for years. Though most were kept to protect my fragile young psyche, this was one of many based on misplaced humiliation and shame.

In recent years, many of the mysterious events of our family's past have been brought out into the light of God's healing. With these insights, I have since been able to fit together many of the scattered pieces of the confusing and chaotic puzzle that lay buried in my memory.

One of the most frightening disturbances for me during this time, shortly before Beth left for the Catholic Charities Home, was the terrible night of the big fight I mentioned earlier. This is one memory I wish I could forget.

Rosie and I shared a bedroom at the time, and we were just drifting off to sleep when we heard our parents in the dining room engaged in a loud discussion. Their voices grew uncharacteristically louder, until they accelerated into shouting. I don't remember what was said, but the tone was frightening, in that it was foreign to hear my parents shouting at each other. We jumped out of bed and stood holding hands in the dark, listening intently at the door. We stood there together as though frozen, in a state of disoriented confusion as we heard our Father whispering, rather loudly, in a pleading voice, for our mother to "please, calm down, before you wake the children."

That's when we heard the sound of shattering glass. Rosie and I ran down the hall and burst into Beth's bedroom. Over the course of what felt like hours, though it was probably only a few minutes, there followed a nightmarish storm of breaking dishes and furniture. And to my utter dismay, I heard the distinct destruction of my mother's precious guitar. Most assuredly my heart was crushed. At some time in the midst of this horror, my brother made his way up the stairs into Beth's room, where we all huddled together on Beth's bed. She held us, like frightened chicks, under her wing.

In the aftermath, when the crashing and shattering stopped, the only sound we heard was Mom's sobs. After a few minutes, Beth tiptoed to the door and cracked it open just enough to peek out. Ever so quietly Rosie, Jack, and I joined her as we crept into the hallway and peered down the stairs.

Our mother sat on the kitchen floor in her nightgown, sobbing into her hands, surrounded by the carnage of broken dishes and furniture. We watched from the top of the stairs as Dad bent down to help her up, and then he held her tenderly in his arms as she wept.

When he looked up to see us peering down, his face held such a look of shame and sorrow that we stepped quietly back into Beth's bedroom and closed the door. When all was quiet and Mom had gone to bed, the four of us padded downstairs, where our Father was sweeping up the mess.

He set aside the broom and leaned against the kitchen counter, looking weary and defeated. Then he began to weep, quietly at first, then in great heaving sobs. I had never before seen my father cry, which frightened me more than the shouting and breaking glass. He just kept repeating, "I'm so sorry. I'm so sorry," as we all huddled around him in one big group hug.

Though he was a gentle, tenderhearted guy, he was truly a "man's man," one who held his deepest emotions in check. Dad was strong and brave and smart, and he could fix anything, yet in that moment he looked like a hurt and frightened little boy, most certainly incapable of fixing this horrific mess.

Though it was never stated openly, certainly not that I was privy to at the time, I had the sense that my mother's relationship with Father Poole was at the center of this turmoil. And though I couldn't see it then, I realize now how incredibly pivotal that night was in my young life. The stability of our family had been on shaky ground for quite some time, yet my father was the rock-solid foundation I depended on to keep us from falling apart. The shock of seeing him in such a vulnerable and broken state was no doubt a catalyst that gave rise to a deep rift in my young soul, one that would rock my sense of security for many years to come.

Chapter Eight
A VISIT TO WARD E

Dammasch State Hospital
Clinical History and Progress Record
7/27/65
PHYSICIAN: Dr. R. Hendow
PATIENT: Martha Mueller
WARD E

Case History

This is a 41-year-old, white, married, female patient whose main complaints were severe emotional disturbance.

Family History

Father alive, 84 years old and under psychiatric care due to severe depression and suicidal tendencies since the death of his wife [Martha's mother]. He had several EST [electro-shock treatments].

[Martha's] Mother died of heart failure. She [Martha's mother] became emotional after marriage due to the passive and lazy attitude of her husband, who left to her the management of all family problems.

Siblings: the patient [one of 14 children] has five brothers [still living] and seven sisters. [The eldest sibling, a boy, died before the patient was born.]

Personal History

The patient had a stormy childhood. Her parents frequently quarreled and were in bad financial condition. All the children lacked hygiene, and the mother treated the patient particularly harshly, probably because the mother took all the responsibility of rearing the children. The patient stated also that she was mistreated by priests and sisters in the [family parish] because of their harsh ways. She finished the 10th grade in school with average marks and had no social life because of poverty and lack of hygiene. When 14 years old, she was molested several times [by an older male family member]. In 1941 the patient was married and this resulted in six children, now ranging in age from 23 to 7, who are physically and mentally healthy. The husband-wife relationship for the first seven years was quite good and then started to deteriorate because the husband was the passive type who left all the responsibilities to his wife, according to the patient, but the patient herself preferred to have a dominant husband instead of her being domineering, which apparently she became. The patient worked as an aide in a private hospital for one year then as a wirer in Tektronix for seven years, but because of the passive attitude of the husband, the patient became frustrated, withdrawn, and depressed. She was seen by a psychiatrist as well as priests for help. Her condition remained fluctuating, confusing, and restless. In 1961 she had a hysterectomy and then she has been treated with hormonal shots and vitamin B 12 ... In early 1965 she became acquainted with a priest who was taking care of her boy in his studies and became romantically involved with him, which made her deeply infatuated and deeply attached to him, although later on the priest moved to Alaska, the patient did not change her attitude and became more agitated, frustrated, also feeling a guilt complex. Finally she was asked by a psychiatrist to be hospitalized ...

Clinical Notes 7/29/65

Patient admitted to ward ambulatory. Is pleasant and cooperative. Seems quite depressed. When asked what color her eyes were she replied, "Sad"

G. Caughlin

Discharge Summary 8/9/65

[The patient] was assigned to group psychotherapy, but she showed no interest, and in the meantime she became bored in the hospital and asked to be released. Which was against my advice, and it was no use to explain to the patient that her short hospitalization was not enough to give any satisfactory improvement, but apparently she was determined to leave the hospital, giving the excuse that she wanted to see her private psychiatrist. I called her husband and explained the situation, but he was helpless in reversing her decision, and I had no choice but to let the patient leave the hospital against medical advice.

Final Diagnosis

Psychoneurotic disorder, depressive reaction; involutional reaction.

Prognosis

Poor.

Dr. R. Hendow

✄ ✄ ✄

In June of 1965, when Jim Poole drove away from our home for the last time, Roseanne and I were just two little kids, glad that school was out and looking forward to the long summer vacation that stretched ahead of us. Little did we realize at the time the long-reaching effects of his influence over our mother and how the course of our lives would be forever changed following his departure.

The summer turned out a lot different from what I had expected. Instead of going camping or to the beach with my family, like in a normal year, Roseanne and I spent the last part of the summer with the family of some of our parents' friends.

The LaVilles were very nice people, lived in a large house, and had about a hundred kids. Actually, I think they had *only* ten, but they were always so busy and noisy that it seemed like there were a lot more of them. They attended our church, which is how we knew them. Because we had been to visit them several times over the past year, it wasn't like they were strangers, but it did feel weird living in someone else's house. Even so, it was kind of like an adventure because everything was so different.

Dad told us that Mr. LaVille had a heart condition that kept him from working a regular job. Instead, he ran a home business, raising small animals, mostly rodents, for pet stores.

Mrs. LaVille was a big woman, which I thought was funny because Mr. LaVille was short and skinny. They were definitely an unusual-looking couple. She liked to cook, and it seemed as though she spent most of the day in the kitchen.

Roseanne and I lived with the LaVilles because Mom went to stay in the hospital for a while. Unlike the other times when she went away on one of her extended "vacations," this time she was in Dammasch State Hospital, which I overheard Mrs. LaVille telling someone on the phone was a mental facility. I guessed my mom was mentally sick, whatever that meant. I just knew that most of the summer either she walked around like she was half-asleep or she would sit and cry. She'd say mean things to Dad when she didn't think we could hear, and all he would ever do was sigh and shake his head. Apparently he couldn't make her happy.

When Roseanne and I went to visit her at this hospital, it was creepy, not at all nice, like the other place where she normally stayed, with the pretty trees and flowers and the cute little apartment. Bars encased all the windows at this hospital, and I was scared of some of the people in there. It was embarrassing when one of my friends would ask me where she was. I didn't want to tell them because they might think she was like one of those crazy people.

❅ ❅ ❅

August 1965

As Dad drove the car down the ramp and onto the freeway, I slouched in my seat, making myself comfortable for the drive ahead. Though I had no way of knowing it at the time, we would make this trip countless times over the next six years. I would come to know every landmark, every bend in the road so intimately that I swear I could navigate the trip with my eyes closed.

Heading southbound on Interstate 5, Dad shifted in his seat and lit a cigarette before settling into the right-hand lane. Staring out the window at the passing cars and tree-lined view of the muddy Tualatin River, Dad, Roseanne, and I passed the time by talking and telling jokes.

After about a half an hour, I glanced up at the sign for the Wilsonville exit. Dad turned off the freeway and we headed down the country road that led to our destination. After a few more miles, several large buildings surrounded by an expansive green lawn came into view.

Encircling the perimeter of the complex of buildings and lawns was a high cyclone fence. As our car turned into the entrance and we passed through the front gates, a large sign welcomed us to Dammasch State Hospital.

"Well, here we are," Dad said while looking at us in the rearview mirror. He combed his slicked-back hair neatly into place. "I want you girls to be on your best behavior."

"Dad, you tell us that every time we go somewhere." I said as we made our way up the shrub-lined path that led to the front entrance of the largest building.

Roseanne shook her head and rolled her eyes. "We're not babies, you know."

Dad pulled the heavy door open. "All right. I just want us all to have a nice visit."

"We will, Dad, don't worry," I said, though I was so nervous I felt like running back to the car.

Once inside, Dad checked us in with the attendant at the front desk. Then we made our way down a long corridor in the direction of the elevator, our footsteps echoing eerily off the high ceilings.

Once inside the elevator, Dad pressed the button for the fourth floor. As we ascended, a knot formed in my stomach. I wrapped my arms around myself in an effort to self-soothe. Looking down at Roseanne, I saw the same nervousness mirrored in her eyes.

When we reached the fourth floor, Dad led us down another long hallway until we arrived at our destination, indicated by a sign on the right side of a pair of large double doors. He pressed a buzzer, and after a few minutes a man in a white coat opened the door, welcoming us into the strange little world of Ward E.

Dad then checked in with yet another attendant. While Rosie and I waited, I scanned the room, looking for Mom. I spotted her seated at one of the many tables. I noticed clusters of people seated with their coffee cups, some playing cards and several others talking quietly with what I assumed to be other visiting families.

Mom looked up. When she saw us, a big smile spread across her face, and she stood to greet us. After several minutes of hugs and kisses, she led us to an empty table. Before sitting down, she went into another room and returned shortly with a tray containing two cups of coffee and two small plastic cups of a weak, sour purple juice of some sort for Roseanne and me.

Mom asked how Roseanne and I were doing at the LaVilles's. We all made small talk as though this were just another ordinary day.

Dad presented her with a carton of Salem menthol cigarettes and a two-pack of Luden's Wild Cherry cough drops. I watched as she puffed nervously at a cigarette. Before finishing with one, she used it to light another. Just as frequently, she would pop a cough drop into her mouth. She offered Roseanne and me each one before tucking the little box back into her pocket.

Sucking on the cough drop, I scanned the room. I tried hard not to stare, and when I glanced over at Roseanne I noticed her eyes darting nervously from one scene in the room to another.

Directly behind us were a row of large chairs, many of them with heavy wooden trays attached. An old woman was locked securely into one of the chairs. She acted out a pantomime of folding, ironing, and sewing before starting in on an invisible knitting project. I watched in fascination. I looked at Roseanne, who was also watching this woman. Wide-eyed, Roseanne returned my gaze and we burst into a fit of giggles.

"She spends most all day doing that," Mom said. "She's perfectly harmless. She seems happy in her own little world." She dismissed our curiosity as she waved away the cloud of smoke between us, frowning slightly at our rude giggling.

"How would you girls like to go see the activity room?" She brightened as she stood up from the table.

En route to the activity room, Mom stopped to introduce us to a few people we encountered along the way. John, a deaf mute, probably in his mid-thirties, signed his request for a cigarette by pressing two nicotine stained fingers to his lips, making a muted half-puffing/half 'uh-uh' sound. Reluctantly Mom offered him a cigarette. While lighting it for him, she looked over her shoulder. "We're not supposed to give him any. But I don't see the harm in it. He is a grown man, you know."

She then introduced us to Little Mary, a small-framed young girl whom I gauged to be roughly my age. Mary was also locked into one of the wooden tray chairs with a cloth belt secured around her waist. Wearing a protective helmet, she repeatedly banged her head against the wall, her arms folded across her chest and her fingers firmly grasping her slip straps.

"Hi, Mawee," she slurred with obvious amusement when introduced. "We hab the same name. Yur mudder is sooo nice!" She squealed and gave a crooked smile, her rocking and banging momentarily ceasing. "She pways her guitaw and sings to me sometime when I can't sweep."

"That's nice." I was unsure of what else to say.

"And this is Roseanne, my youngest."

"Nice to meet you," Roseanne finally said when Mom tipped her head, delivering an unspoken message that Roseanne should offer a polite response.

When we arrived at the activity room, Mom led us through the door. A pool table dominated the room, and in one corner sat a small box-like structure with several round holes cut into the front. On top of the box was a pile of beanbags. Roseanne and I hurried over to it and immediately began a game of beanbag toss, a welcome distraction to the depressing surroundings.

"I'll leave you girls to it for a while, okay?" Mom said as she made her way toward the doorway. "Your dad and I will be right in the other room."

We soon became bored of the beanbag game, so we tried our hand at a game of pool. Mercifully, after about twenty minutes Mom and Dad appeared in the doorway and announced that visiting time was over. Mom walked with us to the door, holding hands with Roseanne and me on either side of her. I sensed her distress at our departure as she tightened and loosened her grip, her palms cold and sweaty.

A confusing mixture of relief and regret stirred in my belly as we approached the large double doors. The resentful adolescent I was becoming wanted to push away and run through the doors to the car, yet my little girl heart wanted to throw my arms around her and cry, "Mommy, please come home!"

When we reached the door, Mom embraced us all, tears welling in her eyes. She reminded Dad to "please bring more cigarettes and cough drops next time you come."

With one last peck on the cheek, we said our good-byes.

As our footsteps echoed throughout the long corridor and around the corner, I heard the sound of the door as it clicked shut, closing in the strange little world of Ward E.

❋ ❋ ❋

Thirteen Months Later

In early September 1966, Mom had been home for several months and we'd actually gone on a few family outings. It was starting to feel like things were getting back to normal by the time school started that year. I was in the sixth grade, Roseanne in second grade, and C.J. was now attending Public High School. Beth was out on her own once again, Joan was happily travelling the world, and Diana was busy taking care of her two little daughters. I dared to think we were a normal happy family. But deep down I feared it would be only a matter of time before Mom slipped away again.

I could see it in her eyes—the way she would stare out the window with a faraway look when she sat at the dining room table, sipping her coffee. *What in the world was she thinking about?*

❋ ❋ ❋

February 1967

Yep, I was right. Mom didn't stay home for very long. Shortly after she left Dammasch, she went to stay at that pretty apartment place called Morning Side for a few weeks in October. Then she went to another hospital called Holladay Park. I overheard Dad telling my sister Diana that he couldn't afford for her to stay in either of these places anymore and that he was quickly running out of money. So shortly after Thanksgiving, Dad took her back to Dammasch

Mom got to come home for a couple days on Christmas and New Year's, but it wasn't all that fun. Usually Mom does lots of baking and decorating, but there wasn't time for any of that. Diana and Aunt Donna each brought over plates of cookies and some homemade candy, but nobody made Mom's special divinity candies or her famous Snappy Turtle cookies.

These were my personal favorites. Not only were they yummy but also great fun to make and especially fun to eat. They look just like little turtles—with a round spicy cookie body and walnut halves for the little arms, legs, and head. After baking the cookie, Mom would drizzle warm chocolate frosting over the top and then let it harden, giving the "turtles" a shiny brown shell. I enjoyed eating them in a certain way: first bite off the arms, then legs, followed by the head. Next I'd lick the chocolate off the shell before biting into the spicy cookie. The best part, though, was making them with Mom.

Chapter Nine
OH, YOU BEAUTIFUL DOLL!

Dammasch State Hospital
Clinical History and Progress Record
PHYSICIAN: Dr. Hendow
PATIENT: Martha Mueller
WARD E

Readmission Note

Date: 11-22-66

This 41-year-old white married female patient is known to us from previous hospitalization as psychoneurotic disorder, depressive reaction. She left our institution on 8-9-65 against medical advice, but as her condition deteriorated and due to financial difficulties, she was advised to return and thus she was readmitted on 12-7-65. The patient herself has not been satisfied with her marriage because of the personality conflict with her husband, who is permissive and protective to the patient.

Several attempts to help the patient by priests and family counseling were of no benefit because of the uncooperation [sic] of the patient.

She had a course of 16 EST [electro-shock treatment] without apparent improvement and was finally discharged on 1-19-66 on condition that she should continue with her husband to attend marriage counseling outside of the hospital. She failed to do this, and recently she has become more acutely depressed and had to be brought back for readmission. Upon interview, she showed the same clinical picture as in the past. She was well oriented and organized in thought. She showed no gross hallucination. She was acutely depressed, in a crying mood, manipulative and hostile towards her husband. Thus, she was readmitted on 11-22-66 and was placed on Stelazine 5 mg. t.i.d. and Kemadrin 5 mg.t.i.d.

Diagnosis

Psychoneurotic disorder, depression reaction.

Discharge Summary

Date: 12-6-66

This 41-year-old white married female patient was readmitted for the third time to Dammasch State Hospital on 11-22-66 because of acute depression. Her marriage to her present husband has not been successful because Mr. Mueller is a passive, quiet, permissive person who has left most of the responsibilities on the patient. This created a feeling of depreciation towards him, and the patient became argumentative and frustrated. Thus, the husband-wife relationship started to deteriorate.... In 1961, the patient had a hysterectomy, which appeared to worsen the condition. Various attempts were tried by psychiatrists and priests to help the husband-wife relationship, but to no avail.... Hospitalizations in the past have proved of no avail with this patient. Chemotherapy has been tried as well as EST. It was suggested to the patient and her husband that temporary separation might be helpful if not a permanent one. This advice was not met with approval by the husband.

During her present hospitalization at Dammasch, the patient has shown no response.... She forced her husband to ask for her discharge in order to carry [on] treatment on private basis outside the institution. Thus on 12-6-66, the patient was discharged from Dammasch to the care of her husband.

Diagnosis

Psychoneurotic disorder, depressive reaction, involutional reaction.

Prognosis

Poor, because of the sad husband-wife relationship and none of them is willing of full cooperation.

Dr. Hendow, M.D.

❄ ❄ ❄

Thanksgiving Day, November 21, 1966, 8 AM

"Wake up, sunshine." The tickly sensation on my cheek stirred me from a deep sleep. Mom's fingertips brushed lightly across my face and through my hair.

"Mmmh" I grumbled softly, rubbing the sleep from my eyes. "Okay, I'm awake." I pushed her hands away and sat up, stretching as I reached down to my toes. "But, hey, there's no school today. Remember, it's Thanksgiving."

"Oh, silly me, I guess I forgot."

By the grin on her face I knew she was teasing, and before I had the chance to respond, she placed a package on my lap. "I have something I wanted to give you." She sat on the bed beside me.

"I wanted to give this to you before the day got too busy with all the cooking and company and all. I know it's still a few days until your birthday." She put her arm around me and cuddled me close. "I just decided to give this to you a little early, if that's all right?"

"Sure." I squeezed the package in my lap. I was feeling excited but also confused and a little suspicious. I'd be turning twelve in less than a week. It wasn't particularly unusual to celebrate early, since my birthday, November 27, was always around Thanksgiving. It was a good time to celebrate when the family was already gathered. But this was definitely different. I'd never received a birthday present in bed before.

As I tore into the wrapping, I wondered what could be so special that Mom would give it to me now, in bed. Pulling back the last of the paper, I looked into the face of a blue-eyed doll. Her eyes, accented by the rosy spots on her shiny pink cheeks, looked demurely away, off to one side. Her soft body was stuffed with cloth, and her hair, gathered into two braids, was a satiny weave of bright pink and white. Her rosebud lips pursed into a pouty smile.

Dressed in a pink-and-white checkered pinafore overlaid with a little white apron, she stood on a platform, about a foot and a half tall. On her feet she wore a pair of simple white buckle shoes.

As I looked her over I was filled with a mixture of emotions. She was cute, no doubt, and I appreciated my mother's thoughtfulness, but still I was disappointed. I hadn't played with dolls since I was very little. Even then, I was more interested in playing in the dirt with my brother's toy trucks, climbing trees, and making forts with the neighbor boys. What I *really* wanted was a horse, but that was probably never going to happen.

"Thanks, Mom," I mumbled as I set the doll aside and squirmed out from under the covers. When I began to gather up the wrappings in a pile, Mom put both hands over mine to stop me.

"I can see that you are a bit disappointed, so I want to explain." She pulled her hands away and patted the bed beside her for me to sit back down. "This is not a doll for you to play with. She is for you to keep nice, on a shelf or on your dresser top. See, you will soon be a young woman and will be too old for dolls and other playthings. So this is the last doll I will buy you. I just wanted to make sure you knew how special she is and, mostly, how special you are to me."

"Thanks, Mom." I said again and stiffened a bit as she hugged me, feeling guilty for not really being more thankful. I climbed off the bed and placed my new doll on the top of my dresser.

"Happy birthday, Sweetheart," she sing-songed and blew me a little kiss over her shoulder as she closed the door after her.

✖ ✖ ✖

Friday morning, November 22

"Good morning, sleepy head." The tantalizing smell of bacon cooking drew me downstairs, where I found Dad preparing to crack an egg into the hot frying pan. "One egg or two?" He poised the second egg over the sizzling bacon grease.

"One, I guess." I rubbed the sleep from my eyes then stared blankly into the open refrigerator. I reached in for the pitcher of orange juice. "Where's Mom?"

"Oh, she decided to sleep in a little. I guess all that cooking yesterday wore her out." He flipped the egg, which sizzled and popped in the hot grease, then shook salt and pepper over the top. "Grab the jar of blackberry jam while you're in there, and"—he pointed with the spatula—"butter the toast, will ya?"

"Make me some eggs and bacon too." Roseanne flopped onto one of the dining room chairs and situated her stuffed elephant, Dumbo, in her lap. She pulled her nightgown over her legs until it covered her bare feet. "I'm cold." She drew Dumbo tighter to her chest.

"I didn't hear the magic words." Dad looked at her over the top of his glasses as he put the plate of buttered toast onto the table. "Go get dressed if you're that cold."

Roseanne heaved a sigh. "Pleeease?" She rubbed her shoulders while shivering. "Where's Mom?"

"Sleeping in, so you'd better be quiet." I pulled on Dumbo's ear. "Let me see him."

"No, he's keeping me warm." She hugged him close, turning her shoulder away from me as though to protect him from an assault.

"Now, knock it off you two, or you will wake up your mom. How many eggs do you want, Rosie?"

"Two. *Please.*"

Dad placed a plate of eggs and bacon in front of Rosie then pulled up a chair and sat across from us.

"Your mom and I are going for a little drive this afternoon." He reached for the jam and began spreading a thick coating over his toast. "I thought I'd drop you guys off at your sister Diana's for the day."

"Goodie!" We cheered in unison. Rosie and I enjoyed spending time at our big sister's and playing with our nieces, Debbie Lynn and Sarah, who, at one and four years old, were really more like little sisters. It was also a lot like having our own live dolls, pushing Sarah around in her stroller and playing hide and seek with Debbie Lynn in their big backyard.

Besides, none of my friends could play today. They were all busy with Thanksgiving weekend family stuff, so I was dreading a boring day at home doing nothing. Diana was a good cook and occasionally she would let us bake a cake or something. Sometimes Rosie and I would walk down the street to the park or the corner market for candy bars if we helped her clean house.

"Finish your breakfast and I'll take you over there as soon as you're dressed. But be quiet. Let's allow your mom to sleep as late as she wants, okay?" Dad took a bite of the jam-laden toast and washed it down with a swig of coffee. He let out a big sigh. His shoulders drooped as he stared out at the backyard while we finished our breakfast.

❌ ❌ ❌

"You guys want to stop for dessert?" Dad said as he pulled the car into the Dairy Queen parking lot. Rosie and I glanced at each other, each with a surprised look of confusion.

"Yeah!" Rosie clapped her hands.

I studied him, suspicious about what had prompted this unexpected gesture of parental benevolence. Dad rarely ever did impulsive things. I couldn't tell you the number of times we begged him, sometimes holding our breath for the entire block before the DQ (as though this would affect his decision), pleading that he "Please, *Please*, **Please stop!**" only to have him drive right on past as we puffed out the last of our held breath in defeat.

"Hey, come on." He punched me lightly on the shoulder and motioned with a jerk of his head toward the building. "Your sister is going to get in line in front of you."

I climbed out of the car and followed him in.

After we placed our orders, Dad led us to the back corner of the dining room. He placed the tray with our desserts onto the table and scooted into the booth across from us.

"So, how was your drive?" I asked, dipping my spoon into the whipped cream on top of my hot fudge sundae.

"Where'd you guys go?" Rosie butted in. "We helped Diana make a big pot of turkey noodle soup. It was deee-lish-us." She slurped the milkshake as some of it slid down the end of the straw when she pulled it from the cup.

"I bet it was. Diana's a good cook, and I heard you guys were a big help to her, keeping Debbie Lynn and Angie entertained. Hey, be careful there, Rosie." Dad wiped at a blob of milkshake that plopped onto Rosie's chin." You gonna drink that, or wear it?"

"Yeah, where did you go?" I repeated Roseanne's question.

"Well, that's what I wanted to talk to you guys about."

I narrowed my eyes as I looked across the table to him. Diving my spoon under the chocolate syrup, I pulled out a spoonful of ice cream and popped it into my mouth. I hoped it would ease the sudden pain in my stomach. I had a vague flashback of a similar conversation about a year before, and I had a sneaking suspicion I knew exactly what he was going to tell us.

"Your mom asked me to drive her back to Dammasch." He blurted it out quietly. He glanced around the room, clearly checking to see if any customers had heard.

Roseanne immediately fell to sobbing softly into her arm, her forehead on the table as she pushed her milkshake away with her free hand. He rested his hand on top of Roseanne's head.

I glared at him. "I wanna go home." I stood, walked across the room, and tossed my sundae into the garbage before hurrying out the door to the car.

We drove home in silence, except for Roseanne's sobbing into Dad's lap as she lay across the front seat. I sat in the back seat, staring out the window into the pitch-dark sky, the knot in my stomach growing tighter with every passing mile.

All the way home I kept thinking about how Mom had promised that we'd make Christmas candy together this year, and my favorite, Snappy Turtle cookies. And next week we were going to get the decorations down from the attic. Dad said he would put the lighted Christmas star he had made years ago onto the roof and string lights across the front of the house.

I also thought back to last summer and how much fun we all had at Mom and Dad's twenty-fifth wedding anniversary party in June. They both looked so happy, and everyone said what a handsome couple they were. Mom had been home this time for almost a year, and I thought she was getting better.

Liar, I thought. Then a pang of guilt hit me, so I reached over the seat as we pulled in the driveway and patted Roseanne on the back. She pushed my hand away. I slumped back against the seat, crossing my arms.

"Fine! 'Scuse me for trying to be nice." Before the car had come to a complete stop, I pushed open the door. As Dad applied the parking brake I jumped out and ran into the house, slamming the front door behind me.

I ran up the stairs, taking them two at a time. I burst into my room and plopped onto the end of my bed. I crossed my arms and shook my head.

I heard Dad and Rosie coming into the house and then Roseanne shuffling down the hall to her bedroom. Through the thin walls I could hear her sniffling in the next room, which just made me madder.

Liar—the word kept shouting in my head over and over. *Big fat liar!* I looked across the room and eyed my new doll sitting on the top of my dresser, where I had left it yesterday.

"Liar!" I growled under my breath through clenched teeth. "'I want you to know how special she is and how special you are to me,'" I mocked my mother as I grabbed the doll off the dresser. My mother's words, spoken only yesterday, burned in my ears. I had a clenching ache in my stomach, and the sour taste of bile in my throat made me want to retch. "So special." I aimed my sarcasm at the doll, noting her coy, averted eyes. "Look at me!" I grabbed her by one limp arm, gave her a good shake, and then pitched her violently across the room. She slid across the top of the dresser, knocking a book onto the floor. With a satisfying thump, the doll fell to the floor, where she slumped onto her face.

"Liar, liar!" I glared at the doll then threw myself on my bed, put my face into my pillow, and sobbed.

Chapter Ten
WHO'S VISITING WHOM?

From January to August 1967, Mom was in an out of the various hospitals numerous times. Dad would check her into Dammasch, then after a couple weeks, or sometimes even just a few days, she would insist on leaving there so she could receive private treatments at Morningside or Holladay Park Hospital.

Though Dad had previously declared that he could no longer afford these private hospitals, he must have found a financial resource. I believe he wanted to do what he thought was best for her, but he usually ended up doing what she thought was best, regardless of the conflicting advice of the doctors at Dammasch.

One disturbing result of the chaos and uncertainty surrounding Mom's comings and goings (which resulted in a lot of my own comings and goings) is that I have sketchy memories of that whole year; however, I have been able to piece together a lot of missing memory from studying Mom's medical records, which document dates and places and the ongoing condition of our family situation. Also helpful has been the information contained in my father's ledger. Dad kept meticulous accounts, including the addresses of where we lived after he and Mom separated in January 1967.

C.J., Roseanne, and I moved with Mom into a small apartment in Beaverton in early 1967 when Mom and Dad separated. It had an outdoor swimming pool, though being winter it was much too cold to enjoy. I also recall sitting at the dining room table playing cards with Mom and Rosie. However, my recollection of this card-playing experience feels more like I was visiting Mom for the day rather than living there. And that is how that whole year felt for me, as though Mom was just a visitor... or was it that I was the visitor in her life?

At this time Dad was advised to complete the court documents to make their status a legal separation in order to protect himself financially. Mom was becoming more and more unpredictable, and Dad was becoming increasingly financially stressed.

Just prior to this, in the fall of 1966, I had attended public school for the first time. I was in the sixth grade at Aloha Park Grade School. I *loved* this school and my teacher. Some of my fondest school memories were of my time there. When I moved in with Mom and had to transfer to an elementary school in Beaverton in January 1967, I was devastated. The safe and comfortable bubble that I remember at Aloha Park burst in an explosion of confusion and frustration. The sense of loss I felt over leaving there was as great or greater in my twelve-year-old world than my parents' separation.

For a short period, Dad moved away from town to work in a body shop in Eugene, Oregon. Though it was only a little over a hundred miles away, it might as well have been on the moon, for it felt to me like he had just disappeared. Though Mom had been in and out of my life for several years and my oldest siblings had moved away and returned only for short stays, Dad was the one constant, reliable person I'd had until then. I could always count on him to be there. His "disappearance," along with changing schools mid-year, further rocked my already shaky sense of security.

In the spring of '67, Dad moved back into our family home, and Roseanne, C.J., Beth, and I moved with Mom into a small house in Beaverton. I ricocheted back and forth between this little house in Beaverton when Mom was out of the hospital then back to stay with Dad whenever she relapsed and returned to Dammasch. By the end of the school year, I had moved back to our family home where Mom and Dad were working to make a go of their marriage once again.

As summer began, I dared to think, even hope, that life would get back to normal (whatever that meant) and we would be a "real" family, like we were supposed to be. We went on a few camping trips and even had some of the students from a local Catholic boarding school come stay with us for a few days at a time—just like in the "old days."

Then in August, when all of life seemed to be happy, normal, and ordinary, the early-morning arrival of an ambulance in our driveway brought my summer fantasy of a happy family to an abrupt close.

❈　❈　❈

August 22, 1967

Lying on top of the bedcovers, I tossed and turned, miserably uncomfortable. The temperature had hit the 100-degree mark at 3 o'clock in the afternoon, and though it was now 10 PM, the air in my upstairs bedroom was unbearably hot and stuffy. Wide awake and restless, I climbed out of bed and crept down the hall.

"You asleep, Rosie?" I whispered as I tip-toed into her bedroom and over to her bed.

"Are you kidding? I feel like a baked potato lyin' here waiting for someone to melt butter over me."

"Scoot over." I chuckled under my breath, not wanting to wake Mom and Dad in the bedroom directly across the hall.

"No way, it's too hot to sleep together!"

I slumped onto my butt on the floor. Drawing my knees to my chest, I leaned back against the side of the bed.

I sighed. "I wish we would have asked to sleep outside tonight."

"Yeah, that would have been a good idea." Rosie sat up on the edge of the bed, her feet dangling next to my head.

"Why don't we go downstairs and sleep in the living room." I yanked her by one foot. "I bet it's a lot cooler down there."

Together we crept down the stairs, and when we reached the bottom of the steps, a deep voice called out of the dark space of the dining room.

"Boo!"

Roseanne squealed and grabbed my arm. We both jumped backward out of the doorway.

"Daddy, you scared me." Roseanne laughed nervously.

"I caught ya' though, didn't I?" He laughed and pulled us both into an embrace.

"Ooh, it's too hot for hugs." I pushed away.

"Yeah, I couldn't get to sleep either," he said, flipping on the dining room lights.

"I suppose you two would like to sleep outside." He pointed to the garage door. "Your sleeping bags are on the bottom shelf."

"Good night and don't let the bugs bite," he teased as we raced across the room and out the door.

"Love you, Daddy," I called over my shoulder.

"Me too," Rosie echoed.

He winked. "Close the door quietly. Don't want you guys to wake up your mom."

Now fully awake, I unrolled my bag onto the soft green lawn in the backyard. I stretched out on top of my bag and a flutter of excitement filled my belly. It was still too hot, even outside, to even think of climbing inside the bag. With bent arms, I pillowed my head in the palms of my hands, wiggled my bare toes, and gazed up into the night sky.

Rosie sighed. "Aren't the stars pretty?"

"I love sleeping outside," I said in a hushed voice, as a warm breeze tickled my bare arms and legs. "Let's see if we can find the Big Dipper." I felt like a tiny speck lying there in our little backyard under that big starry sky.

After about a half hour, the air began to cool enough so that we climbed into our sleeping bags and finally drifted off to sleep.

✄ ✄ ✄

As the first pale morning light began to turn the sky from deep black to dark gray, an increasing awareness of the hard ground under my back brought me fully awake. A large pebble was poking into one of my ribs. As I opened my eyes, I felt the puffiness in my right eye where a spider had bitten me. Morning dew lay over the lawn and my pillow-less head. It was then that I remembered what I didn't like about sleeping outside.

"I'm going back in the house." I said to Roseanne when she began to awaken.

"Me too. My back hurts." She crawled out of her sleeping bag.

As we made our way through the garage, which had a door that led into the house, I noticed through the large garage door windows a light flashing at the front of the house.

"Hey, what's with the flashing lights?" Just then I noticed a different flashing light. This one was red.

Roseanne and I rushed into the house, through the kitchen and dining room, and into the front hall. Dad stood by the front door, at the light switch, flashing the front porch light on and off. He startled when he heard us and turned around.

"You girls, go back outside and go back to sleep." He tried to admonish us, but his voice was oddly weak.

We were way too wide-awake for that.

"What are all the flashing lights?" Roseanne pushed past Dad and peered anxiously out the front door window.

I joined Roseanne at the window, but Dad pulled us both away as he opened the door to the two uniformed men, who stepped into the now very crowded front hall.

"She's up there." He pointed up the stairs. "Last door on the right."

"Daddy. *Daddy!* " Rosie struggled against Dad's efforts to herd us into the living room and prevent us from following the ambulance attendants up the stairs.

"What is going on?" I was nearly shouting, dazed in confusion, my heart racing with the terror I saw reflected on Roseanne's face.

"Sit down and listen to me." Dad's quiet but firm command was strained. With eerie calmness he pressed us both firmly onto the sofa. "Your mom is not feeling good this morning, and these men are going to help her."

Grasping Roseanne's chin firmly in his grip, he forced her to look him in the eye. Her eyes, wild with fear, darted past him, attempting in vain to see what was happening up the stairs.

I sprang up, trying to follow the uniformed men, but Dad blocked my attempt. He shoved me gently back onto the sofa.

"Listen to me!" His commanding tone got our full attention. He kneeled in front of us.

We pleaded with him to please let us go upstairs and be with Mom.

"It's going to be all right." But his words failed to assure us.

I heard crackling, mysterious radio code talk as one of the men rushed down the stairs and out to the vehicle. He returned carrying a stretcher, which he expertly maneuvered up the stairs all the while continuing his radio communication.

Roseanne whimpered. "What are they doing now? I want my mommy"

I stared in horror after the attendant. A surreal feeling of this is just like on TV made me start to giggle.

"It's not funny!" Rosie punched me in the belly.

"I know it's not funny. Hey, that hurt!" I felt my face heat in shame and frustration. I hugged myself around the waist.

Seconds later the three of us jumped up as one as the men with the stretcher made their way down the stairs. Dad stepped in front of Rosie and me, though he was unable to keep us from darting around him and rushing to Mom, who lay pale and still on the stretcher.

I was horrified to see that she was unconscious. When I tried to shake her awake, Dad pulled me away.

"Is she dead?" I demanded to know.

"Mommy. Mommy." Rosie clutched one of Mom's limp hands. "Don't be dead"

"No, honey, she's not dead. These nice men just gave her something to help her sleep." Dad pulled Roseanne and me away from the stretcher.

The men made their way out the door and down the front walk. They placed Mom into the back of the ambulance as the three of us stood on the front porch, Dad on his knees with his arms around his two sobbing daughters. We watched the vehicle, the reflection of the lights turning the neighboring houses a garish shade of red, until it turned out of sight and the wail of the siren faded into the distance.

Chapter Eleven
HOME NOT-SO-SWEET HOME

On the morning of August 23, 1967, as the ambulance whisked my mother away, I had the terrifying thought that I might not ever see her again. However, my fears were relieved later in the day when we learned that after she had been delivered safely to St. Vincent's Hospital and was treated for an overdose of tranquilizers, she would indeed live.

The next day she was then transferred to Dammasch State Hospital, where she was officially court committed. This attempt to end her life was just one in a series of various episodes over the course of the next few months, which included cutting her wrists, throwing herself down a fifteen-foot concrete stairwell, and another overdose of pills.

Shortly after her commitment date, at the beginning of the 1967–68 school year, Roseanne and I met with one of Mom's doctors for a family conference. During this meeting, the adults (Mom, Dad, and the doctor) presented to Rosie and me the possibility of our staying for a while with a nice family from our church. They made this idea sound so fun that by the end of the session I was ready to go home, pack my bags, and prepare for a new adventure.

The adjustment to being in another strange home and yet another school, not to mention that it was my first year of junior high, was almost beyond my ability to cope. I turned thirteen shortly after we moved in with the McDougall family. At the onset of my teen years began another startling loop of the roller-coaster ride my life had become.

November 28, 1967, Beaverton, Oregon, McDougall Family Residence

Reclining on my bed, I leaned back against the wall and stared up at the pink-and brown-checkered curtains that framed the bedroom window. *How nice those colors look together. I never would have thought of that combination.*

Rolling onto my stomach, I stroked a hand across the pink and brown floral design on the chenille bedspread, noting with approval how pretty it looked against the pale pink walls. How strange this room felt. Nice, comfortable, and pretty—my own, but not my own.

On the bed beside me was a little heart-shaped wooden jewelry box. Lifting the lid off the little box, I put it to my nose, taking in the strong aroma of cedar, which stirred a warm and pleasurable sensation in my chest.

Yesterday was my thirteenth birthday, and the little box was from my sister Diana, who had come for a short visit—just long enough to deliver her gift.

Holding the lid up to the light, I examined the intricately engraved brass flower design, which served as the handle, and smiled with admiration at the deep brown marble at the flower's center.

Rising from the bed, I made my way across the room while thinking how much I had enjoyed Diana's visit. I missed my family, my real family. I sighed and placed the little heart box on top of the chest of drawers then picked up the bottle of perfume Mom had given me last week when I had gone with Dad and Roseanne to visit her at Dammasch.

The bottle was shaped into a bud vase—a shiny translucent, deep red color. Pulling the rosebud-shaped stopper from the bottle, I poked a finger into the top then dabbed a little of the perfume behind my ears.

To a Wild Rose wafted throughout the room, reminding me of Mom. She had sold Avon products for years, and this was one of her favorite fragrances.

As I replaced the stopper, I sighed.

"I really miss you, Mom," I whispered as I set the bottle-vase next to the little heart box.

I then began rearranging the things in the room, enjoying the luxury of a few moments of privacy in the midst of this busy, boisterous family.

I was still trying to get used to the noise and activity in this big house with ten people all under its roof. Even though I had grown up in a large family, only the three youngest children had still been at home the last few years.

Roseanne and I had moved in with the McDougall family just a few weeks prior, and it still felt strange being here.

Everything was so different from what I had been used to growing up. In my real family, I had three older sisters, one older brother, and one younger sister. This family had five boys and only one girl, Linda, who was nine, the same age as Roseanne. In my real family I was the fifth child. In this house I was a few months older than Danny, the oldest of the six McDougall siblings. The youngest boy, Timmy, was just four years old.

Although strange, it felt kind of nice to be the oldest. I had a few special privileges. Danny and I got to stay up later than the younger children did, and it was nice that I had a bedroom all to myself. Roseanne shared a bedroom with Linda.

I continued to rearrange the things in my room. I stopped when I noted the cloth doll Mom had given me last year, on my twelfth birthday.

"You have the sweetest face." I cooed to the little doll, holding her at arm's length. "And such bright blue eyes and rosy cheeks. I remember when Mom gave you to me." I reminisced, with a mixture of sadness and warmth, what Mom had said. *This will be the last doll you will receive from me. Soon you will be a young lady and too old for dolls.*

"Well, right now I don't feel too old for dolls," I said to the sweet little face. Alone in the privacy of my bedroom, I held her to my heart.

I lowered myself onto the edge of the bed and rested my chin on the doll's head. A tear trailed down my cheek and splashed onto the skirt of her pink dress, followed by one more, then another... until my chest constricted into heaving sobs. I felt as though my heart was breaking.

After a moment the sobs quieted. I heaved a sigh while considering how everything felt so confusing, being here and away from everything and everyone familiar. Hiccupping, I began to rock the doll in my arms, moaning softly between broken, ragged breaths.

I had experienced so many changes in the last few years, but always I had been with my real family. Even if they were messed up, at least I knew who they were and that they loved me. At least I thought they did. At this point I wasn't so sure anymore. In fact, I didn't know about anything anymore. I began crying again and sobbed into the little doll's pink dress.

But I do know I don't want to be here in this house with all these people. All I really want is to go back home to my real home with my real family. Sniffing into my sleeve, I hugged the doll tighter still. *Maybe if I write and tell Mom how much I miss her, she'll try harder to get well and come home.*

Using the palm of my hand, I brushed away the tears and jumped to my feet. I tossed the doll onto the edge of the bed. As I crossed the room, the doll slid, forgotten, onto the floor.

Sitting at the writing desk under the window with the pretty checkered curtains, I reached into the drawer for a pen and paper. With a loud sniff, I wiped my nose with the back of my hand and began my letter.

Dear Mom….

❃ ❃ ❃

"Dinner's ready!" The familiar evening announcement was a welcome interruption. After finishing my letter to Mom, I had been sitting at my desk reading my seventh grade Social Studies assignment, "The beginning of the Industrial Revolution in America."

This is so boring! I groaned, rereading the same paragraph a third time. It was so uninteresting to me that my mind continually drifted to other things.

Thank goodness Christmas was in just a few weeks. That meant two whole weeks of vacation and no stupid homework. I tossed the book onto the desk and answered the call to dinner, relieved for the distraction.

"I'm coming," I called out as I made my way down the hallway toward the dining room. Several voices echoed my answer, and the thundering of footsteps trotting up behind me in the hall ensued. The front door opened and slammed shut followed by shouts and stomping feet charging up the front steps toward the dining room.

Children came from all directions of the house to the dinner table, bumping into each other, some laughing, others squealing or shouting, each jockeying for a position at the table.

"Quit pushing me!" "That's my spot, Dad. He's in my chair." "Make him move." "Oh goodie, pork chops!" "Yes! I love pork chops." "Hey, Mom, where's the gravy for the potatoes?"

"Everyone sit down and be quiet," Jack shouted in his deep baritone. "Mary, you sit here. Danny, you sit there." He motioned to his right and left sides.

"Keep your elbow in," Danny reminded me and smirked as I settled into the seat to Jack's left.

Jack grinned mischievously as he held up his dinner fork, stabbing at the air in the direction of my right arm and Danny's left, warning all diners to keep their elbows in tight when eating at this crowded table. "How convenient that Mary is right-handed and Danny is a Southpaw."

Giggles echoed around the table at Jack's joke as I felt the heat rise to my cheeks. Swallowing my embarrassment, I rolled my eyes and joined in the teasing banter, lifting my right elbow out in mocking fashion for Jack to jab then pulling away before his fork could make contact.

As everyone settled into their seats, an unspoken signal caused a hush to fall on the room. Jack looked around the table with a stern warning at each of the eight children assembled, followed by a wink and a pleased little grin. Glancing at his wife, Ladonna, she grinned and winked back, releasing an exhausted sigh.

"Bless us, O Lord, and these Thy gifts, which we are about to receive," Jack bellowed. "From Thy bounty through Christ our Lord."

A chorus of "Amen" punctuated the prayer and then like a dam that had burst, a cacophony of voices flooded the room. "Pass the potatoes." "Hey, don't hog all the gravy." "Mom, this is delicious." "Where's the green beans?"

And so it continued throughout the remainder of the meal, until all bellies were full and desert was served.

Savoring the last spoonful of chocolate pudding, I glanced across the table at Roseanne. We had been here just short of a month and were beginning to settle into the routine of this busy family. I was grateful to have Rosie here with me. It helped me not to feel so much like an outsider.

Roseanne returned my glance with a wistful, somewhat nervous smile. Mealtimes were stressful for her. She was having a hard time getting used to the noise and competitiveness in which this big family conducted their meals. I sensed her anger at the way Jack teased me and tried to assure her that I could take it.

I also noticed how Roseanne spent a great deal of the mealtime with her head down, her eyes darting nervously around the table, and seemed only to pick at her food. Years later she confided in me that she usually left the table hungry. She found it difficult to eat because of the tight knot in her stomach. She would often sneak into the pantry in the evening to snack on handfuls of parmesan cheese, raisins, crackers—whatever she could find that she could scarf down covertly while the rest of the family were downstairs watching television.

When Roseanne and I had first arrived at the McDougall house, we were allowed a bit of time to get used to our new surroundings; therefore, not much was expected of us concerning chores and such. But one night around the dinner table, all that changed.

"Mary, starting this week, you are to wash the dishes after dinner on Mondays and Thursdays," Ladonna announced. "David, Tuesday and Friday; and, Danny, Wednesday and Saturday. I will do them on Sundays. You've been here nearly a month, and you are thirteen years old now, plenty old enough to take on the responsibility of helping out around here."

I sighed but knew it wouldn't do much good to argue. The boys were happy with the arrangement, though. They had to do this chore only twice a week instead of three times now that I was there to share the work, and I felt the resentment growing within me.

Everyone had their assigned daily chores and a schedule of who did what when. The younger children took turns at setting and clearing the table. On Saturdays there was a whole other list of weekly duties.

Ladonna motioned to me from the kitchen. "Come on in here and I will show you how I load the dishwasher." As the other family members made their way to various parts of the house, Jeff and Brad began clearing the table, snickering behind their hands at my obvious contempt.

Standing beside Ladonna, I slumped impatiently against the counter. Looking through the kitchen window, I watched Danny push his brother Timmy on the backyard swing, enjoying the last few minutes of the evening twilight. Ladonna droned on about how to prepare and load the dishes.

I wish I could ride my bike around the block before it gets totally dark. I turned my attention to the counter cluttered with dirty dishes and pans. *I'll bet I'll never get to watch any TV tonight either. And I still have that stupid Social Studies homework to finish.*

As the stack of dirty plates grew higher and higher, I began drumming my fingertips on the countertop.

"Pay attention!" Clearly irritated, Ladonna raised her voice as she bent down to grab the dishwasher soap from under the sink.

Grumbling under her breath, she went down on her hands and knees to retrieve the box from the back of the cabinet, where it had been carelessly tossed onto its side. With her fingertips she swept the little pile of spilled soap into the palm of her free hand then tossed it into the garbage pail under the sink.

"I have a lot of other chores yet to do tonight, so let's get this one done." She grasped the edge of the countertop and hoisted herself upright. Wincing, she pressed the palms of her hands into the small of her back as I continued staring out the window, tap-tapping my fingers, in an impatient rhythm.

"Have you heard anything I just told you?" Ladonna snapped.

"Yeah, Yeah, I got it!" I felt heat rush to my face when I sassed her. "No problem."

"All right then, I'll be back in a while to check on how it's going." Ladonna sighed in obvious frustration. Walking away, she shook her head slowly, clenching and unclenching her fists as she made her way down the hall.

The boys had finished their table-clearing task, so I was now left alone to do my job. Taking a deep breath I surveyed the kitchen, perturbed at the overwhelming stack of dirty plates and the seemingly endless rows of drinking glasses and serving dishes.

I'm gonna be here all night. Reaching for a dirty plate from the top of the stack, I felt hot tears stinging at the edge of my eyelids. Methodically, I began rinsing each dish under the faucet and arranging them into the bottom of the dishwasher.

Starting on the drinking glasses, I began to relax as I moved into a rhythmic pattern. As I cleared the countertop of the dirty dishes and filled the dishwasher trays, I was surprised to feel a sense of satisfaction.

I sighed, relieved to be finished. *That wasn't so bad.* I wiped my hands on the dishtowel that hung on the oven door. *Maybe I'll get to watch some television after all.*

"I'm all finished," I said just as Ladonna stepped into the kitchen to check on my progress.

Glancing around the room, Ladonna sucked in a deep breath. She seemed to force a wan smile. Furrowing her brow, she shook her head. She opened the dishwasher door, nodded her apparent approval, noting the pots and pans soaking in the sink-full of soapy water, just as she had instructed. She nodded again.

I watched her inspection impatiently. Glancing at the clock, I noted it was just a little after seven o'clock. *Just enough time to watch one hour of television and still have time to get that stupid Social Studies homework done.* I was relieved that the evening wasn't a total loss.

"Pretty good job," Ladonna said. "But you forgot to wipe down the countertops." She frowned as she handed me a wet dishrag.

Taken off guard at the unexpected criticism and my last bit of patience exhausted, my temper shot out of control. I threw the dishrag into the sink full of soapy water. "That does it! I'm tired of being treated like a slave!" I crossed my arms and puffed out my chest. "You never told me I had to wipe the counters! Forget it. I'm done. I'm going to watch television!" I stomped toward the doorway.

"Get back here, young lady, right this minute!" It seemed Ladonna would not give in to a stubborn thirteen-year-old's tantrum.

I stopped in the doorway and turned back to face the kitchen. Taking a deep breath, I narrowed my eyes and glowered. "It's not fair. I did just what you told me and now you are changing the rules!"

"It's just common sense, Mary. Look at those messy countertops. Just come back in here and wipe them down and you'll be all finished." Ladonna softened her voice, clearly trying to diffuse the situation.

"You do it. I'm not your slave!" Throwing one last glare over my shoulder, I stormed out of the kitchen and ran headlong into Jack.

"Is there some kind of a problem here?" Jack's booming baritone frightened me. He looked me square in the face

I stepped back and swallowed hard.

"It's not fair! She never told me I had to wipe the counters off. I'm not doing it!"

"Well, we'll just see about that."

I felt the weight of his large hands on my shoulders, forcefully turning me around. With his not so gentle push between my shoulder blades, I stumbled back into the kitchen.

Jack stood silently at the doorway while Ladonna handed me the dishrag. She gave an imploring, weary look and then stood beside her husband.

I felt the heat rising in my face as I franticly wiped down the countertops.

"Don't forget to wipe off the table too." Jack instructed from his post at the doorway. At least his voice wasn't quite so booming, but I was smart enough to realize that he wasn't going to take any lip from me.

Hot tears ran down my cheeks as I did the task.

When finished, I glanced over at the pair in the doorway. They both nodded their silent approval. Tossing the dishrag to the back of the sink, I turned my back as Jack and Ladonna stepped out of the room.

I glanced up at the clock and swiped at my tears. Almost seven thirty. Fuming with frustration, I stomped out of the room and down the stairs where the other children were watching television.

Charging into the TV room, the evening's program was already underway, I was greeted with "Shh!" "Be quiet!" "Turn it up." "I can't hear." and other irritated reactions to my disruptive entrance.

"What's your problem?" Danny glared at me as I rustled the stack of newspapers piled onto the one vacant seat in the room.

"None of your business!" I tossed the newspapers onto the floor, scattering them in disarray.

"Fine. What do I care anyway." He rolled his eyes and turned his attention back to the television.

Roseanne glanced over at me. She wore a frown, but it was not of disapproval but of concern.

I answered with a smirk and a dismissive wave of the hand. Then letting out a loud puff of breath, I shook my head and turned my attention to the television.

My breathing began to return to normal and I forgot about the clash over the countertops as I became engaged with the television program. I settled deep into the comfortable easy chair and lost myself in the images on the screen.

"...And now, a word from our sponsors," the program's host announced.

Jumping from the chair, I shouted, "Dibs. I get my place back!" and hurried toward the bathroom. David tried to crowd in front of me, but I beat him there by one stride, slamming the door in his face.

When I returned to the TV room, my anger shot up a few notches. "Hey! I said dibs. I get my place back." With my hands on my hips, I stood before Danny, who now occupied my chair.

"Too bad, you got up. Now it's my chair."

"But, I said dibs! That's the rule. When you say dibs, you're supposed to get your place back!"

"Well, maybe it's *your* rule, but it's not here in our house. Isn't that right?" He nodded toward his siblings seated around the room.

"Please, just let her have her seat back," Roseanne said. "Then we can finish our program."

"Yeah, gimmie back my seat." I kicked Danny's shin.

As if I were invisible, Danny peered around me at the television.

That's when I began kicking him increasingly harder and faster.

After about ten seconds of these irritating kicks, Danny jumped to his feet and shoved me, nearly knocking me over. "Knock it off! Just sit down over there and shut up!" He pointed toward the empty chair across the room.

When I pushed back, Danny lost his balance and grabbed the arm of the chair to right himself. He exploded back toward me. He puffed his chest and drew up within inches of my face, his breath rapid, loud, and barely controlled.

"Sit down and shut up!" he said between clenched teeth, while forming his hands into tight fists.

"Try and make me." I was primed for a fight. I pointed my chin in the air.

Then I turned to walk away, but before I took a second step, Danny reached out and grabbed my bra strap.

As I yanked away from his grasp, something seemed to break loose inside my pent-up emotions.

It was at just that moment that Ladonna stepped into the room, probably aroused by the shouting voices.

"Don't you ever grab me again!" I was enraged by this violation.

"Settle down, Mary." Ladonna had raised her voice just enough to get my attention.

"Yeah, right, go ahead and take Danny's side. You always do anyway. What do I care. I hate you! I hate all of you! I hate this stupid house. I hate being here. I hate you! I. Hate. You! I HATE YOU!!!"

I ran out of the room and up the stairs. I threw open the front door. Outrage propelled me as I continued running down the front walk and out to the sidewalk.

Heading blindly toward the main street, the slap of my tennis shoes stomping against the pavement kept time with the blood rushing in my ears.

Where are you going? a voice inside my fevered mind asked.

What do I care! I thought, running even faster. *Anywhere, I don't care. Just away from them, away from that house, away from all of those stupid people!* My thoughts screamed in my head.

I ran until my legs burned and my lungs felt like they were on fire. Then I ran farther still. Tears streamed down my face and I gasped for breath.

Finally the pain in my side grew so intense that I stumbled onto my knees. Doubling over, arms clamped around my ribcage, I gasped for air before plopping ungracefully onto my bottom. I sat on the sidewalk and wrapped my arms around myself in a desperate embrace.

I sat there and wept in angry abandon. "Mommy, Daddy, I miss you so much, I want to go home." I wailed into the cold night air. "I want to go home."

As I sat on the cold pavement, I released deep sobs from my heart. I felt as though I could curl up right there beside the road and rock myself to sleep. But soon the cold, damp air began to seep through my thin, sweat-dampened T-shirt, and I began to shiver uncontrollably.

I stood slowly to my feet and started walking back in the direction I had come. I didn't know where else to go. I felt utterly defeated. Sniffling and sighing, head downcast and feet scuffing the sidewalk, I didn't notice the approaching car until it pulled alongside me.

Through the open window I heard Jack's voice. "Hey, Kid, you need a ride?"

I forced my lips into a weak smile as I made my way around to the passenger side. "Yeah, sure." I quietly surrendered as I slid into the passenger seat. "Why not?"

Thankfully, Jack was quiet on the drive back to the house. He pulled the car into the driveway, and I jumped out as soon as the car stopped. I ran up the front walk and pushed open the door, grateful that no one was in the hallway as I slipped quietly down the hall to my bedroom. Alone in my room, I noticed my doll on the floor, where I had tossed her earlier. Picking her up, I slipped under the covers, cradled her gently to my chest, and wept myself to sleep.

Chapter Twelve
ADOLESCENT ANGER AND TEENAGE ANGST
LET THE PARTY BEGIN!

I n spite of myself, I did survive living with the McDougall family. I'm also happy to report that they apparently survived living with me as well.

Though I definitely did not appreciate it at the time, I now recognize that my time with them was the last period of stability in my life for many years to come. It must have been a great relief to my weary father to know that Rosie and I were being well cared for while he worked, attended to Mom's needs, and cared for his own needs.

Though I missed Dad greatly, I knew that he loved us. I believed he would eventually come back for us, which he did in August 1968, when Mom was discharged from Dammasch.

In the year that followed, Mom once again hopscotched between coming home on trial visits and readmitting herself back into what appears to me now as the security of Dammasch. While reading through Mom's records of her stay during this period, I couldn't help but chuckle when one aide's "insightful" report states the obvious: "Martha seems to do quite well while here but does not seem to be able to function well in society."

Over the course of the next two and a half years, she was admitted, both voluntarily and involuntarily, four more times.

She even moved out on her own for a period of time, into an apartment in downtown Portland and worked as a nurse's aide. Sadly, this attempt at independence ended in her taking yet another overdose, thus resulting in her return to Dammasch.

On April 20, 1969, her forty-fifth birthday, after a two-month trial visit, she readmitted herself. Less than a month later, on May 16, while on a day pass with either Beth or Diana, Mom acquired numerous pills from various pharmacies. Noted in that particular admission report, "Martha took enough pills to make herself Blotto."

As I read through these accounts of Mom's comings and goings, I found myself at times cheering for her whenever I read the rare, encouraging, hopeful remark. These were written by aides and occasionally by a doctor who truly seemed to care—who seemed to look past the surface of her behavior and see into the truly wonderful person that (I know) she was.

I also found myself railing against the naysayers, those who continually predicted her failure and judged her as selfish, hopeless, and doomed. And I was truly incensed when I read one particular doctors' comments, judging my strong and loving father as being weak and passive. His report glibly advised that "he should try his best to change his attitude, to be more active and take the job of the master in the house, no matter how the patient responds to this new attitude."

And while all of this was going on with Mom, Dad, Roseanne, and I were working our hardest to live our lives as best we could. C.J. had enlisted in the Army in March of 1968. Our four-bedroom house on two acres was way too much for Dad to keep up by himself, so he rented out our large home and moved us into a series of smaller, low-rent houses and apartments.

Surprisingly, I managed to stay in the same school from seventh through ninth grades, but the disruption of moving so many times greatly unsettled me. Though I finished ninth grade at Highland Park, by the end of that year my grades were so bad, I was really wasting the teachers' time. I was there only because I had to be. I was miserable, sullen, and restless—the perfect storm of angst and rebellion, just waiting for trouble. I aligned myself with a group of like-minded misfit friends and walked around most of the time with a giant chip on my young shoulders.

During eighth and ninth grades, since Rosie and I were no longer living in foster care, when Mom was away and Dad was working until at least 5 or 6 each night, Roseanne and I became what was cleverly coined as latchkey kids, which basically meant that we came home after school to an empty house. This often resulted in after school parties, which consisted of neighbor kids coming over with beer and cigarettes stolen from their parents. It was also a great opportunity to explore and experiment sexually. Though we did spend time during the summer months picking berries or staying with relatives and friends who had parental guidance, for the most part we pretty much ran wild. This was definitely the period for Roseanne and me that my oldest siblings referred to as being "raised by wolves."

My need for acceptance and physical affection led me into numerous shameful sexual experiences, including two incidents of date rape when I was fourteen. With boys my age, I never went "all the way," but just far enough to hear them tell me they loved me, words that most every love-starved fourteen-year-old girl yearns for and most fourteen-year-old boys know how to use to fulfill their cravings. These experiences invariably elevated the boy's status when he bragged to his buddies in the locker room the next day. Conversely, by the end of the day, I was labeled a slut, a whore, an easy lay. Has anything changed since then?

Since this was the era of drugs, sex, and rock 'n' roll, I had no problem finding and experimenting with a vast variety of drugs, including my gateway drug of choice: airplane glue. I also discovered that the spray used to seal charcoal drawings in art class did the job, as well as lighter fluid, nail polish remover, and various other toxic chemicals. It was only by God's grace that I didn't kill myself or at the very least cause permanent brain damage while experimenting.

If I back up just a bit in my drug history, I must also include my very first drug: Dramamine, an over-the-counter motion sickness medication that has the pleasant side effect of causing drowsiness.

Whenever a school counselor could convince my dad to come pick me up because I was just too "sick" to remain at school, I would down a couple of these straight from the medicine cabinet and sleep away the rest of the day in peace and quiet. And like magic, the whole crazy, confusing, and painful world would *poof!*—go away for the next few hours.

Once I discovered the powerfully effective and emotion-numbing comfort of those chemicals, I moved on to marijuana, acid/LSD, peyote, and psychedelic mushrooms. A girlfriend with a "nice" older brother (who date raped me) was only too happy to introduce me to and supply me with whatever I was game for. The one place I drew the line was shooting up heroine. I was terrified of going there. However, the areas I was willing to venture into proved to be equally dangerous.

Chapter Thirteen
THE PARTY'S OVER
OR
DID YOU KNOW YOU COULD GET PREGNANT FROM SITTING ON A FIRE HYDRANT?

October 1969, Beaverton, Oregon

Shortly before my fifteenth birthday, I was sitting on top of a yellow fire hydrant in front of the Taco Time on Beaverton-Hillsdale Highway when I first met Gary. It was a Friday night, and my friend Diane and I were at the Valley Plaza Mall, which back then was the best place in town for hanging out. The mall consisted of a movie theater, an ice skating rink, a bowling alley, a couple fast food restaurants, and a few little shops.

Dad had dropped us off about a half hour earlier and said that he'd be back to pick us up at nine. That meant we had about two hours to see what kind of trouble we could stir up. Though we were supposed to be bowling, when we didn't see anyone we knew there, we left. That's how we ended up in front of Taco Time, with me sitting on that yellow fire hydrant, eating a bean-and-beef burrito, watching the traffic go by.

And just as our luck would have it, two cute guys happened along, drove in off the highway, and pulled up in front of my fire hydrant. The guy in the passenger seat rolled down his window. I immediately noticed his curly brown hair and nice smile.

"Hey there." He winked at me. "How would you girls like to go to a party?"

I looked over at Diane, who shrugged her shoulders, like she could take it or leave it.

"I'm gonna go in and get us something to eat," Curly Hair informed his friend then strolled ever so casually into Taco Time. As he walked past us, he gave me a long appraising look, running his eyes up one side of me and down the other, all the while flashing that nice smile. Then he tipped his head in a little nod of approval. After he went into the building, I jumped down from my hydrant and walked over to Diane, who was busy talking to the car's driver.

"I'm Dan." He reached a hand through the window, which Diane gave a little shake.

"Hi, I'm Diane and this is Mary." She giggled.

"Hey, Diane." Dan looked over at me. "Hey, Mary." He tilted his head toward the Taco Time. "And that's Gary."

I gave Diane a little kick in the side of her leg then shot her a look that I'm certain she knew meant "Whadda ya think? Should we go or not?"

She just shrugged again, so I knew it was up to me to decide. A few minutes later we are on our way to a party.

I was eager for the excitement, the adventure, and, most of all, the attention and affection Gary showered on me so that I'd willingly fulfill his needs. I eventually found out that I was just one of several girlfriends he had during the "dating" period of our relationship—that is if dating means sneaking into my bedroom at night, or going to friends' homes where he'd get so drunk he almost killed us both driving in that condition. Maybe it was a date the night I drank so much wine so quickly that, surprisingly, I did not die of alcohol poisoning. However, I was so sick over the next two days, I could barely get out of bed to go to the bathroom. Did that qualify as a date?

Even after I discovered Gary's other girlfriends, I was so shamefully desperate for affection, I convinced myself that he was sincere when he promised to end it with them. I knew he hadn't, but my need was so great and my self-worth so low that I chose to pretend it was true.

And for the next few months it was one party after another, until late in the summer of 1970 when the party came crashing to an abrupt end. I was pretty sure that I was pregnant, and this pregnancy was no small problem. I was only fifteen years old and had just graduated from ninth grade. Gary was eighteen, but at least he had finished high school and had a job at a gas station. My future job prospect was looking like motherhood.

After I missed my first period, Gary tried to talk me into ending the pregnancy. I wasn't having any part in that, and after briefly considering putting the baby up for adoption, I ruled that out as well. My older sister Beth had done that with her first baby.

And even though we never discussed it, I knew it was a huge heartache for her. I wasn't willing to make that decision.

So in July 1970, four months before my sixteenth birthday, I was two months pregnant. My mother was locked up in the state mental hospital, and my dad was about ready to pull his hair out trying to deal with Roseanne and me and our wild ways. At least my brother was easier to keep track of, since he was in the Army, and my three older sisters were all married and off his worry list.

So Gary proposed this really romantic idea. "I guess we ought to get married, then." He said this as he ran his fingers through his hair and sweat dripped from his forehead and down the back of his neck—though it wasn't from the heat.

We were sitting on the shady back deck of his parents beautiful Hillsdale Heights home when he "proposed" to me. A slight breeze provided a teaser of relief from the heat.

"Well, we need to talk to my dad first." Just thinking about that, I felt little butterflies of nausea flit in my tummy. I wrapped my arms around my waist and bent over, letting out a little burp that threatened to send my lunch onto the deck.

Talking to my Dad wasn't as hard as I thought it would be. He had figured out that I was pregnant. He probably knew before I did. I guess that's what comes from fathering six kids. Those early morning sessions in the bathroom didn't slip past his radar. Even though I tried to cover up the sound effects with running water and flushing the toilet, he knew.

And when Gary brought up the idea of our getting married, Dad just sighed and said that he would sign his consent,[1] stating, "I might as well sign for you, Mary, cause if I don't, I know you'll just move in with him. At least this way you will have legal protection, and the baby will be given a name."

We married in early September and set up house in a dumpy apartment. By Christmas we had moved into a cute little one bedroom, 1940s bungalow-style house in a suburban neighborhood of Beaverton. Gary was working afternoons and evenings at the gas station, and he had gotten a second, early-morning job with NW Natural Gas Company.

❆ ❆ ❆

January 1, 1971

We married in September and before the end of that year, we moved three times: packing, unpacking, decorating, and moving again. I had also celebrated my sixteenth birthday and spent Thanksgiving and Christmas with my new husband and his family.

I spent most of my time alone at home, waiting: for Gary to come home late at night, for my next doctor's appointment, for someone to call or drop by, which rarely happened, since all my friends were in high school. Mostly, I slept and waited for my baby, due March 4.

Some days when the weather was nice, I would walk up the street to the City Park and sit on the swings or on a bench and watch the mothers with their children, dreaming about what it would be like to be there with my little one come spring.

I also thought a lot about my friends in school—high school. Junior high was such a drag. But I did think that high school might have been fun. Before my life shifted with this pregnancy and subsequent marriage, I had been looking forward to being on the swim team. And I truly missed my friends. They were all too busy to call me anymore. And when we did talk... well, we didn't have much to talk about. All they wanted to discuss was what was happening in school or with this boy or that party.

Oh well, who needs them. I'll have plenty to do when this baby comes. But for now it's boring being home alone all day. Hopefully, after the baby comes, I can get my driver's license and then I won't be stuck at home all day. In the meantime, I stayed home—waiting, watching TV, and sleeping... a lot.

❆ ❆ ❆

February 1, 1971

Gary received a letter from the draft board, stating that he was to report for his draft physical in two weeks. I was anxious about this pending event, and I couldn't help but worry about what would become of the baby and me if Gary had to go into the military. Of course, I was concerned for him going to war in Vietnam. But he kept telling me not to worry, even though I knew he was.

It didn't help my mood much that he would go out drinking with friends when he got off work most evenings. He didn't take me with him. Though this bothered me, I reasoned that because I was so tired all the time, I was pretty much in bed by the time he got off work anyway. It was only about a month until the baby was due, but it felt like forever.

I daydreamed about the baby a lot. *What will it look like? Will it be a boy or a girl? What shall I name it?* But mostly I thought about how nice it would be to love and hold it and to keep me company.

My son Jason Allen entered our lives on February 22, 1971, at 8:32 AM. Gary had arrived home the night before around midnight. I woke up when he crawled into bed and couldn't get back to sleep. I kept thinking, *Just two more weeks until the baby's due.* And then I started having these annoying cramps. I tossed and turned for about two hours, and when they became more intense, I realized I was probably in labor. I woke Gary and we started timing the contractions as the doctor had instructed. Finally around 4 AM, Gary took me to the hospital.

I could hardly believe that I was finally a mother. The birth had happened so fast. It hurt a lot, especially right before he "popped out." But soon after he was born, I started thinking that it wasn't so bad. Gary's parents, my dad, and Roseanne came to see us that evening. Shortly after they left, a nurse brought Jason (my son!) in for me to hold. I fed him a bottle and he fell asleep in my arms. It seemed my dreams of having someone to hold and love had finally come true.

Little did I know then how weary I would become in the days ahead filled with dirty diapers and midnight bottle feedings and the countless hours I would spend alone pacing that little house with a tiny crying baby I felt helpless to comfort.

Immediately following Jason's birth, Gary's mother thought I should go home with them for a few days so she could help me adjust and rest up while she helped to care for the baby. Deep down I resented that it wasn't my own mother. I felt self-conscious with Jeanette. But I didn't feel I had much choice in the matter.

I believed I was ready for taking care of a baby; however, deep down I was terrified. Though Gary's mom was nice and kind, I wished I could've had my own mother with me.

Sadly, I have to admit that for the most part, I really didn't think a lot about my mom. She'd been in the hospital for so long by then, I guess I had gotten used to her not being around anymore. I felt ashamed that I didn't miss her more. It makes me sad when I remember how I thought something must've been really wrong with me, because I should have missed her more.

I tried to console myself with such thoughts as I have this new baby to take care of now. I'm sure that I'll be plenty busy and won't have a lot of time to think about stuff like missing (but not really missing) my crazy mother, or about what will happen to me/us, when/if Gary goes into the military... stupid thoughts.

April 1, 1971, Gary went for his draft physical and received his draft notice shortly after. He was ordered to report to Fort Lewis, Washington, on May 20. His parents offered to let me move in with them for a while. Though I wasn't thrilled, I resigned myself to the idea. Don't get me wrong, they were very nice people. It just felt strange being in someone else's house. I would use Gary's old bedroom, which was downstairs. It was roomy and private. By then I was used to moving around. So what's one more move? I tried to make light of my anxiety.

In the meantime, as we counted down the days before Gary's induction, we shared the remaining weeks of our time together in our little "honeymoon bungalow."

❈   ❈   ❈

April 11, 1971, Easter Sunday, 10:00 AM

Dad and Roseanne were due to come by any minute. I was planning on going with them to Mass at St. Cecilia's Church. I loved Easter. It's such a beautiful time of year, with all the spring blossoms and daffodils and tulips blooming everywhere. I was excited about getting out of the house, and I was looking forward to Easter dinner at Aunt Donna and Uncle Ray's after church.

I sat by the front room window, watching for Dad and Rosie. I allowed my thoughts the luxury of drifting back to better days—

how Mom used to sew matching dresses for Roseanne and me, and how we would go to Roger's Dime Store and she would buy us each a pair of white gloves, a straw purse, and a new hat. We would shine up our little white patent leather shoes, and off to church we'd go. Did we look adorable or what? I sighed with pleasure at the now seemingly so long ago memory.

Then I recalled the ever-popular Easter egg hunt and a big ham dinner either at our house or at one of our aunts and uncles'. Roseanne and I always woke up at the crack of dawn and tip-toed down the stairs. And right outside the door would be our Easter baskets. We'd take them up to our room, crawl into bed together, and start wheelin' and dealin'—making trades for what we didn't like and what the other did. We'd be sick to our stomachs from all that sugar by the time Mom got up to make us all breakfast.

But that had been a lot of years ago. I shook myself from my little daydream and stood to get Jason's diaper bag so I could be ready to go as soon as Rosie and Dad pulled up.

After Mom got "sick," things hadn't been the same, but Dad always made us go to church. That day though, I wanted to go to church. I was so sick of staying home alone all day every day, I was nearly beside myself with excitement, any excuse to get out of the house for a while. Jason was a good baby, but he wasn't exactly great company for a lonely sixteen-year-old girl. Like most newborns, he mostly slept, pooped, peed, and cried to be fed. Thankfully, he didn't cry a lot, and when he did sleep, I would usually pace the house or watch TV or take naps. When the weather was nice, I would put him in the stroller and push him up the street to the park. It was pretty boring, though, since he was a long way from being old enough to romp around on the playground equipment.

So when Dad's car pulled into the driveway, I was ready to go. I picked up Jason and grabbed his diaper bag. But when I opened the front door, Dad stood there, with Rosie at his side, and told me to go back into the house. They came in and sat on the sofa. That's when I noticed that they weren't dressed for church. I knew by the look on his face that something was wrong. Terribly wrong.

"I'm ready to go," I said.

"We won't be going to church. It's your Mom."

My immediate thought was that she had taken a bunch of pills again and that he was going to have to go to the hospital to see her. She did that a lot, took pills, got her stomach pumped, or whatever they do, and then she'd be depressed. Then we'd visit her.

She'd ruined my fourteenth birthday party doing just that. She'd been home on a weekend visit and found a bunch of pills and took them. Dad had to take her back to the hospital during my party. He'd pulled me aside and said, "I need to take your mom back to the hospital 'cause she's not feeling so good."

I had known what that meant, and I was pretty mad at her for doing that to me.

But it wasn't that this time.

How I wish it was.

"Your Mom died last night." He blurted it out, just like that.

I felt frozen in place, my mind struggling to fully comprehend his words.

Roseanne broke down crying. Dad did too. Then I think I did too. Deep down, before he said anything more, I knew that she did it to herself. She killed herself. *She finally did it.* Yet it didn't feel real.

Over the next couple of days, we had to do what felt disgusting to me at the time. One task was going to the funeral home to choose her casket. While Dad, my sisters, brother, and I were in the coffin room, I studied the various styles. I was appalled by all the frilly, satin-lined, fancy coffins. I couldn't take it, so I hurried from the room, my thoughts chasing me. *It's stupid to spend all that money on a box that you're going to put a dead person in and then put it into the ground for them to rot in! Disgusting!*

I went out to the car and held Jason while he slept. I remember thinking that there must be something seriously wrong with me because I didn't feel sad, like I thought I should be. Instead, I was angry... but at who, at what? I couldn't say.

So I did what Roseanne and I used to do when we knew we were to quit laughing and get serious. I thought about sad things, like dead kittens, until I made myself feel sad enough to cry like I was supposed to. My sister Joan came out to the car, where she saw me crying. She climbed into the backseat with me and put an arm around me. Then I felt better.

The next couple of days were very busy. The funeral was depressing—I guess that's the way funerals are, though. I especially hated the lies about how she died. The obituary in the newspaper said she had died of heart failure. Well, I guess your heart does stop beating when you kill yourself. No one wanted to mention that little detail, but, clearly, everyone knew about it.

You see, I was taught in catechism that it's considered a mortal sin to take your own life and that there would be no place in heaven for you. But the last time Dad made me go to catechism class was when I was fourteen. He'd dropped me off in front of the building, and I'd walked down the hall, out the back door, and never went back.

I clenched my fists. *I don't buy that mortal sin stuff or any other Catholic teachings, so I know she is in heaven.*

Regardless, the funeral was sad, and it didn't help that the weather was rainy and dreary, typical of Portland in April. Even so, I was happy that my entire family was together for the day. I was especially glad the Army had let my brother come home for the funeral, even though he was really pissed off about the whole thing. Seeing my brother in his uniform made me think about Gary having to leave for the Army in a few weeks, and that didn't help cheer me up any either.

I've always felt that it was strangely ironic and rather creepy (though I am not superstitious) that the funeral fell on April 13, Roseanne's thirteenth birthday. The horror of this pain-filled memory of "celebrating" that day has continued to haunt her ever since. With each passing year, Roseanne struggles with a fresh mixture of disturbing emotions.

She sent me the following, in an email dated April 14, 2013, with the subject line "The Day After." That she wrote it in third person is a strong indication of the intensity of the pain she feels, even yet, over that day.

After having a very nice day and evening, I went to bed and later woke up from a horrible dream where I was walking around empty streets and buildings, realizing that all the people were gone and I was the only one left on earth. I had this deep, deep sense of loneliness and despair. Not sure why that decided to hit after such a nice day, but after I was awake, I had this memory about when Mom died and wrote it down. It's sad, but I wanted you to know how I remember it.

The adults thought, "How horrible that her mother killed herself and the funeral is on her birthday." They gave her a cake and sang 'Happy Birthday' while she stared at the candles, feeling shocked and horrified at the attention. No one acknowledged her pain and confusion, and no one consoled her. She wanted to cry, wanted to scream, wanted to crawl in a hole and never see these people again.

But her sister Mary was with her, and she didn't feel so alone. They sat by the brick fireplace that day, and they shared the experience of feeling their mother visit them there. She told them she was in heaven and it was okay. They both felt it and heard what she said, they talked about it to each other, and it was their forever secret.

Chapter Fourteen
AFTERMATH

I n the months and years following my mother's death, not only was I faced with her loss, I was in the process of learning to be a mother myself. Less than two months before her death, at the tender age of sixteen, I had given birth to Jason.

When Gary began his military training in May 1971, I moved in with his parents for a few months, which was extremely difficult for me. Though they made every effort to make me welcome, I felt totally out of place. In physical distance, I was not far away from my family and friends, maybe twenty miles, but I felt utterly alone. Because I didn't have a car, not even a driver's license, I was completely dependent on these people, who were total strangers to me.

When the Army sent Gary to Korea in January 1972, I moved back home with my Dad and Roseanne, until Dad remarried—one of Mom's dear friends, Betty, in August of that year.

I will be forever grateful for the opportunity that those few months afforded me to be close to Dad and especially to Roseanne. She and I were each experiencing our own deep sense of abandonment over the loss of our mother. But my loneliness was compounded by feelings of total rejection and desertion by my husband, Gary. Not once did he write to me during his time overseas. We were never together again after he left for Korea. Though we were legally married for nearly two years, in actuality our marriage had lasted only a few months.

During the time that I was living with Dad, Rosie and I shared a bedroom in the tiny house he had bought after selling our beautiful big house to our sister Diana. The room was just big enough to squeeze in a double bed, which we shared alongside the crib that Jason slept in. I remember most nights spooning with Roseanne, sometimes with Jason between us. We comforted one another as we rocked ourselves to sleep, remembering the sad song our mother had sung to us about the two babes lost in the woods.

When Dad and Betty married in July 1972, I moved into an apartment in Beaverton. I was working at the Beaverton Pharmacy, which had an old-fashioned soda fountain. I served coffee and ice cream to local businesspeople on their breaks, alongside the taxi drivers who sat at the counter while waiting for fares to call on the row of pay phones located in the hallway beside the drug counter.

It was here that I met Jim, a handsome young pharmacist. He was my Knight in the Shiny White Coat, who promised to rescue me from my loneliness. He swept me off my feet by dropping off bags of groceries on my doorstep, along with the occasional bouquet of flowers.

Once we married in June 1973, his greater deeds of heroism included paying off my lingering hospital bill, still outstanding from Jason's birth nearly two years prior. And when Gary relinquished his parental rights, Jim legally adopted Jason. Two years and four days after our wedding, I gave birth to Benjamin.

In less than four years, between the ages of fifteen and nineteen—essentially my teen years—I experienced a whirlwind of one life change after another. In the intervening years between my first pregnancy at fifteen and the birth of my second son at age nineteen, I was married, gave birth, lost my mother, divorced my first husband, remarried, and gave birth to a second son. During this time I estimated that I moved at least ten times.

I would like to say that I then lived happily ever after with my Knight in the Shiny White Coat. Although we did have many happy memories, my emotional needs were far greater than his emotional ability could possibly meet. The ultimate result for me was many more years of a different kind of loneliness.

As challenging as it was for me to raise two sons at such a young age, I must give a lion's share of the credit to my sisters Diana and Beth. They were both raising sons very close in age (and geography) to both of my boys. Without their loving and patient mentoring, I honestly don't know how I would have managed. I was more fortunate by far than many teen mothers, for had it not been for the loving support of my family, I may have ended up just another statistic on the streets, in a homeless shelter, or worse.

As it was, I still had a great deal of difficulty in raising my sons. The legacy of generations of mental illness left a deep mark on my young psyche. And though I am no longer plagued by the guilt and shame I once carried, because I am now covered by the forgiving grace of a loving God, I did pass along the damaging effects of our family's disease, born of abuse, neglect, mental illness, and chemical dependency.

Thankfully, by God's love and grace, along with the help of counseling, appropriate medication, and the support of 12-step programs, I and my sons have found varying degrees of healing. Though an ongoing lifetime process, "recovery" is fraught with the occasional setback along with many triumphant victories. To quote an axiom from AA's *The Big Book*, my sons and I are each "Trudging along the Road of Happy Destiny."[1]

But the story doesn't end here. Let me take you back to the legal battle we were still fighting after three years from the outset.

Part Three

�

Chapter Fifteen
DEPOSITIONS AND THE DAVENPORT

From: Roseanne Miller
To: [Siblings] Diana, Joan, Beth, C.J., Mary
Sent: Tuesday, February 19, 2008
Subject: Letting you know

Dear Diana, Joan, Beth, Jack, and Mary,

I wanted to write you all and let you know that as part of the suit I have filed against the Catholic Church, their lawyers may contact you. I want to let you know that you do not have to talk to them or respond to calls from them outside of a deposition for which they may subpoena you.

It was not a lighthearted decision for me to file this case, and it grieves me that you would have to be involved in any way with this. This is something that I am doing for my own healing and moral conviction to shed light on the wrong that was done to me and to many others by the Catholic Church organizations who did not protect me and others from sexual abuse and have attempted to cover up the truth.

I am not asking for any of you to be involved in any way, and I understand that we all have our own way of perceiving, processing, and keeping what has happened in our lives and in our families. I want to respect your way of keeping it and apologize for any way in which my need to go through with this case interferes with your privacy.

I think we have an incredible family. We have all had our share of hardships, and we are all strong and resilient. I value my relationship with each and every one of you.

If you would like, you may contact my attorney with any questions. He would be happy to address any concerns you may have.

With Love,
Roseanne

From: Joan Miller
To: Roseanne Miller
CC: Diana, Beth, C.J., Mary
Sent: February 19, 2008
Subject: Letting you know

I will cooperate in whatever way I can.

It pains me to think that you feel that you have to actually ask for support from us, as if it would be a great inconvenience. Isn't support to a sibling—especially considering your circumstances at seven years old—shouldn't that support, understanding, and sympathy, anything it takes... be a given? I wish I had been there for you when you were that little girl, but I'm here for you now. I'm so sorry for what happened to you at such a precious age. I can't imagine the fear and mistrust that must have carried over into your life from then on. Nothing can repair that damage. But legal damages?—yes, let's make them pay!!!

I encourage everyone to see the Academy Award–nominated documentary *Deliver Us from Evil*, which is now available on DVD.[1] The scale of criminal behavior in the Catholic Church is massive and [this film] will give a perfect understanding of Father Poole and his cronies—from Beaverton, Oregon, right up to the Vatican. This amazing boys club has been likened to the Mafia.

My love and respect,
Joan

❊ ❊ ❊

The Davenport Hotel, Spokane, Washington

Inspired by restauranteur Louis Davenport, the Davenport Hotel has been world famous since it opened in September 1914. "Gilded with gold, sparkled by crystal and illuminated throughout with 'electrollers,' it was as grand as the finest ocean liners of the day." It was designed by an "up-and-coming architect Kirtland Cutter ... Cutter offered a Mission Revival style theme. The white stucco walls and red tile roofs stood in marked contrast to every other building downtown." Davenport and Cutter wanted it to "represent the world to Spokane [Washington] and be Spokane's welcome to the world.... Cutter designed spaces inspired by great architects of France, England and Spain. Davenport filled them with fine art, songbirds and prepared to seat his guests at tables dressed in the finest Irish linens from Liddell (whose linens sailed on the Titanic).... Ever since opening day, the hotel has promoted itself as one of America's exceptional hotels. It still does. It's still true."[2]

❊ ❊ ❊

May 15, 2008, The Davenport Hotel, 9:00 AM

My knock on the door of room 405 was met with a weak and croaking, "Come in."

As I made my way across the hotel room, I kicked aside a balled up sock then stepped around an open suitcase, its contents spilling over the sides. Strewn across the room were two days' worth of clothes, shoes, and dirty dishes from last night's room service. Just as I was about to sit on the edge of the bed, I was halted by the unmistakable odor of illness.

"Wow, Rosie, you look like death warmed over."

"Yeah, thanks, and I kinda wished I were dead right now. I feel awful!"

Roseanne sat propped up in bed with a container between her knees—an ice bucket that bore the gilded monogram of the Davenport Hotel.

"I've been up most all night." She groaned, clutching her belly.

Leaning forward, I brushed back a stray hair from her forehead, making sure to breathe in through my mouth. "What happened? Food poisoning? Flu?"

"You know, I think the stress of the last few days, weeks actually, finally hit me. I tried to eat some dry toast and tea this morning, but I'm afraid that didn't stay down either."

"Do you still feel up to the drive to Montana?" I pushed aside the empty breakfast tray and sat down on the edge of the bed. Brushing away a few toast crumbs, I stared absently at the bed covers, fighting my own urge to be sick.

We were planning to drive to the Bitterroot Valley, just south of Missoula, later this morning. A friend of mine had kindly offered the use of one of her mountain-top guest lodges in Stevensville, where we would spend a few days relaxing after the ordeal of our time here in Spokane.

"Yeah, I think I'll be fine. Lexi can drive if I need her to. She should be here soon. Then we can get going. I'm anxious to get out of here and put this all behind me."

Roseanne's adult daughter Lexie, who lived near Spokane, would be accompanying us on our mini vacation in Montana. The three would then drive back to Spokane together, and then Roseanne and Beth would fly home.

The last two days had been a stark contrast of extravagant elegance and stressful angst. The hotel was truly palatial, a soothing oasis from the emotional, gut-wrenching, and draining inquisitions that were the deposition proceedings held at a nearby office building.

During that weekend, Beth and I were the last of the six Mueller siblings to undergo questioning. Roseanne had sat for her deposition six months earlier, in November 2007, and the other three siblings in the months just prior to Beth's and mine. These were performed by and at the request of the attorneys for the Church. Several of Roseanne's attorneys were also present to offer their support and counsel over the course of the two days.

Though certainly not stated as such, it appeared to all of us that the purpose of these interrogations was to lead us into saying something the defense would use to oppose Roseanne's claims, to discredit her or find some loophole that would benefit their defense.

Though the formal proceedings, broken up into several sessions, lasted only about two hours each, the entire weekend was wrought with tension before, during, and after the actual deposition meetings.

The evening before the meetings began, Roseanne, Beth, and I went to dinner with Roseanne's attorneys, who briefed us as to what we might expect during the proceedings and encouraged us to think about events of our lives during the time that fathers Poole and Duffy were involved with our family.

This was especially painful for Beth, as it brought up the sorrow and regret of her decision (influenced by Jim Poole) to give up her daughter for adoption. I struggled greatly with the fragmented, confusing, and fuzzy memories of my childhood. To this day I still have a complete loss of memory of some portions of that time. Perhaps it's somewhat normal for a fifty-four- year-old woman trying to recall her life at the age of ten to twelve years old. But I felt particularly frustrated because I so wanted to remember not only for my own peace of mind but for the benefit of Roseanne's case and for the vindication we were hoping to bring to our mother's reputation.

When questioned about our mom's emotional state in the early '60s, Beth said, "It was very upsetting, because up until that time, she was an amazing mom, homemaker, [and] community leader. And it was very upsetting to see the first stages of her falling apart."

When asked to clarify what she meant by "what happened to Mom," Beth's simple yet poignant response was, "Just her whole downfall, her whole cascade into the darkness that she went into."

Questioned further, "Is there a sense... that part of this fall, this cascade into darkness, was the result of her relationship with Jim Poole?"

"I think it was extremely devastating to her, because she was such a completely obedient, devout Catholic that she put the priest in a role of God. And she put her trust in him [Jim Poole]. And he betrayed that trust," Beth said.

The attorney paused before continuing. "Do you blame Poole for the problems your mother suffered during the last years of her life?"

"I can't really put [the] total blame on him, because there is a whole lifetime of things, you know, that happen to [a person], but [if] something triggers that downfall, you can take a person who's weakened by life and you punch them, and…."

One question that especially stood out to me upon reading the transcript of my deposition was, "During the time period that Duffy and Poole were in your home, did you ever notice a change in the way Roseanne acted and her demeanor?"

"[No] I was not aware of [anything about her demeanor]. I was [only] as aware as any ten-year-old would be."

In the intervening moments between our meetings with the Church's attorneys, Beth, Rosie, and I spent time in the hotel lobby visiting with one of Roseanne's attorneys, one of several legal representatives advocating on Roseanne's behalf, a very pleasant and compassionate woman with a heartfelt interest in the plight of victims of abuse, in particular, victims of sexual abuse within the Catholic Church. The other side of her personality on the behalf of her clients was her bulldog relentlessness.

She was there to talk with us before and after our interviews, helping us to sort through the conflicting emotions, questions, and confusion these meetings created.

Of particular frustration to me were the questions regarding where and with whom I was living during the time that my parents had originally separated. As I mentioned earlier, this part of my childhood is blurry, and, try as I might, it still seems to evade my recall. She assured me that it was normal to have spaces of lost memory, especially during times of great upheaval.

I also shared with her my survivor guilt. Why didn't I know? Why didn't I help? And hardest of all (though I am so grateful it didn't happen): Why didn't it happen to me too? Then another disturbing thought arose (certainly not the first time). *Maybe it did happen to me and I have just buried it so deep in my subconscious that I can't remember.*

She assured me that if I was supposed to remember, it would come naturally. She figured that I was just a "happy, secure kid," busy climbing trees, riding my bike, and living life. I was not the insecure, clingy little girl that Roseanne was at that time.

"Predators know how to skillfully seek out and select victims that are the most vulnerable, and you just didn't fit the profile of the prey they were looking for," she said. (See Appendix A for more information about the "Predator-Victim Dynamic.)

This made a lot of sense. "Though I still feel so sad that I wasn't there for Rosie back then."

The attorney rested her hand on my arm. "This too is a very normal feeling."

At this point, Roseanne, who had been quietly listening, interrupted. "Would it help if I shared a little from my perspective?"

"Absolutely," I said. I shifted in my chair and turned my full attention to Roseanne. "Please do."

"Do you remember that little game Father Poole used to pay with us?" She held out her hands, palms up. "Where we would face him, put our little hands on top of his, and try to pull them away before he turned his palms down and slapped us?" She slapped her hands in the air in front of her, "hitting" the imaginary pair.

"Oh, yeah, I always tried so hard to win, but he was usually way too quick for me." I chuckled at the memory.

"Well, I hated that game. I wanted so bad to win. You and C.J. always seemed to be having so much fun with that, goofing around and laughing it off when you got slapped, but not so for me. I wanted to quit, but he wouldn't let me. On one particular occasion, he slapped me especially hard, and it really hurt. As I look back I now see that this was his way of sending me a message—that he was very powerful."

Roseanne closed her eyes for a few seconds, took a deep breath, and shook her head, as though trying to shake off the memory.

The attorney and I listened intently as Rosie went on.

She narrowed her eyes. "And there was a look that accompanied that slap. He stared me right in the eye and seemed to say, 'This is the way it is.' That slap and that look became a defining moment for me, one that totally shook my attachment foundation. Here was a person who everyone thought of as so good, treating me so bad. So, who do you trust if you can't trust a priest?

"I remember all of a sudden being terrified of him, and I felt like the world didn't know or care. It was so confusing. For God's sake, he was like the Pope. It was held out as such a high honor that he was our friend, so special and spiritual. He always seemed so interested in each of us kids. He was charismatic and handsome, and, in spite of myself, I really liked him."

"Of course, we all liked him." I huffed a disgusted sigh.

"And, Mary, as far as you wondering why didn't you know? The funny thing is, I thought you did. He was so covert and crafty that he was even molesting me while you and C.J. were in the same room. One time when he was babysitting us, we were all watching TV in the living room. He made me sit on his lap. I didn't want to, but he gave me 'that look,' and I knew I had to obey him. In my little seven-year-old mind, I thought you guys knew what he was doing to me and that you must have thought it was okay because you never said anything. So as confusing and upsetting as it was for me, it never crossed my mind to tell anyone. I felt so ashamed, yet I didn't understand why. Deep down I believed that I was bad."

Another point that Roseanne's attorney discussed with us during these debriefing sessions was an issue that had come up in Rosie's case regarding the lack of documented evidence of Father Poole's involvement with our family, in particular his alleged visits to our home. When the subject came up of these home visits, she asked what I most remembered about them.

"One of the visits I most clearly recall, with great fondness, I might add, is of an evening when he presented a slide show of his time in Alaska. The images of the native people and the landscape shots were truly remarkable. To this day I can honestly say that while viewing those slides, a desire took root within me to one day travel to this remarkable land."

"Hmm. Do you remember him talking about the Dollar-a-Month Club?"

"No, I sure don't. What's that?"

"It was one of the fund-raising ventures that went on as part of a priest's mission," she said. "While not actively on the mission field, it was common to be doing these fund-raisers while on sabbatical. The Dollar-a-Month Club was a catchy way of allowing a lot of people to give a little to support a big cause." (See Appendix B, "Papal Secrets Policy" and Appendix C to learn how the Dollar-a-Month Club was part of the Church's cover story for Jim Poole.)

"Nope, never heard of it."

The conversation moved to other matters.

✂ ✂ ✂

The drive to Stevensville, Montana, took three hours, and by the time we arrived at our guest lodge, Roseanne was feeling much improved, though she kept her souvenir ice bucket within reach on the floor of the front seat. Though I had previously spent time at this lodge on numerous occasions, my enjoyment was heightened and refreshed in sharing this special place with my sisters and niece as I showed them around the historic building.

The Grist Mill, originally built in the mid-1800s, had been beautifully restored and renovated by a local family in 2002 into a private guest lodge. It was with a slight sense of irony that we read a framed historical document on the great room wall, which stated that in the early part of the 1800s, Jesuit priests introduced flour milling, Montana's first industry, at St. Mary's Mission [a few miles from where we were] in the Bitterroot Valley.

Once we all were settled into our respective rooms, I took a few moments to wander about on my own, browsing the guest library and breathing in the feeling of peace that permeated the air around me. The atmosphere truly reflected the sentiment of the welcome plaque on the front door: "And He said to them, 'Come away by yourselves to a secluded place and rest a while'" (Mark 6:31).

I pulled a book from a shelf and dropped into the chair in front of the antique secretary's desk that stood against one wall. As I glanced distractedly through the introduction of the book in my hands, my eyes were drawn to the open page of the large Bible lying open on the desktop. But what truly caught my attention was a replica of an antique quill pen resting on the open pages. Before I picked it up, I looked down and made note of where the tip of the pen pointed. As though it were a laser pointer, this passage fairly shouted up at me:

> *"No weapon formed against you shall prosper. And every tongue which rises against you in judgment, you shall condemn. This is the heritage of the servants of the Lord. And their righteousness is from Me", says, the LORD.* (Isa 54:17 NKJV)

As I reread the passage, a profound sense of God's presence filled me with joy. I knew He had drawn me to this passage as a way of reassuring me once again that He was truly with us in this battle. The past few days had been filled with question after question, all with the underlying purpose of tripping us up in our words, giving our opponent, as it were, a weapon to use against us. And here was a promise from my Heavenly Father that He would be with us in this fight and that the righteousness of our cause would be our heritage, to be known for generations to come.

I hurried to share this with my sisters, who also expressed the same profound sense of God's loving assurance that He would continue to stand with us in the days and weeks to come.

❊　❊　❊

We spent our time at the guest lodge resting, taking long walks, and enjoying meals together. Over dinner one evening, conversation turned to reflections of our dad and his many virtues.

"You know, he was truly a remarkable man," I said. "Just think about this: with only an eighth grade education he managed to pull off the big American Dream. Six kids all in private schools, the beautiful new house, totally middle class all the way. And, yeah, I know we weren't rich or anything but, you've got to admit he made a great life for us."

Beth got up and began clearing the table. "And remember the dance lessons?" She did a smart little plié, all the while holding my dirty plate gracefully before her. "Those weren't free, you know."

"Yeah, I remember. Very nice plié, Miss Mueller." I gave my best imitation of the namesake of Miss Anita Pianove's School of Dance.

Beth curtsied primly as Roseanne and I applauded in ladylike fashion.

"Funny you would mention that," I said. "Cause that just reminded me of something I've been meaning to ask you all. Did I tell you about the box of Dad's stuff that Nancy (our stepsister) gave me a while back?"

Rosie and Beth both shook their heads, a look of obvious interest on both of their faces.

I got up to help Beth with the dishes, but she motioned me back into my chair. "Sit down and tell us about the box of stuff!"

"Yeah, do tell!" Roseanne said.

"Well, in it was a bunch of cards and letters he had saved, mostly ones that we kids had sent him over the years. He even made copies of some of the letters he'd sent in response. Most of those were ones he'd sent to you, Rosie, when you asked him to tell you about Mom, requesting to see her medical records." (See Appendix G, "The Girl and the Garden," Dad and Rosie's correspondence.)

"Hey, I'd like to see those if you don't mind sending them to me. Okay?" Rosie made me promise to get those in the mail soon.

"But one of the coolest things I found in the box was a bill ledger Dad had saved. It was dated from 1965–1976. Like I was saying, we know that he had a very limited education, but, in spite of that, this ledger was organized and thorough. And his handwriting was impressively neat. He kept track of every penny he spent. I mean, he practically noted how much he spent on chewing gum every month. What reminded me just now was Beth's mention of our dance lessons. Along with school tuition and tithes to the church, Miss Anita Pianove ranked right up there as an important expense."

Rosie dipped her spoon into the bowl of chocolate ice cream Beth had passed around the table. "So what else was noted in this ledger?" A keen interest filled her voice. "Was there any mention of what Amy kept referring to as the Dollar-a-Month Club?"

"Hmm, I don't remember anything like that. But now you've really piqued my interest. When Nancy first brought that stuff over, I spent an evening nosing through it, and then I put it away in a storage closet, intending to go through it more thoroughly at a later time. I guess now's as good a time as any."

"Well, get it out and go through it as soon as you get home, and see if there's any mention of any of that. It may be an important record that could be of use in my case."

❈   ❈   ❈

I was keen to get home, not only to begin going through that musty old book of my father's accounts, but I was most eager to spend some quiet time with my husband and best friend, Lee. We had reserved a room at our favorite B&B for the weekend after my return from Spokane.

I had come home from Spokane exhausted, bewildered, and emotionally spent. And though the two days with my sisters at my friend's retreat were helpful in processing what we had been through, the time away with my beloved was truly a healing balm to my body, mind, and spirit.

I kept thinking of a phrase that Beth used in her deposition to describe our mother's decline from a happy, healthy homemaker to a depressed, drug-addicted victim of suicide: "Her whole downfall, her [long, slow] cascade into the darkness" and how I should write a book and title it *A Sudden and Brilliant Emergence into Light*.

Though I doubt I will ever write that book, it was during my time of reflection at the bed and breakfast when the seed was planted that began my journey into writing this book.

How naïve I had been at that moment. Had I known then what I know now, I might have chosen, though not nearly so catchy a title, something like *The Long, Steady Unfolding of My Past*.

Granted, there have been moments of clarity and brilliant flashes of insight throughout this process, but, for the most part, this journey has been, and continues to be, an ongoing process of healing and discovery.

Chapter Sixteen
MY FATHER'S LEDGER

May 20, 2008

Shortly after Lee and I returned home from our B&B getaway, I began a careful and scrutinizing examination of Dad's musty ledger. With the now yellowing pages, its initial entry, dated January 1965, lists the following expenses:

January 1965	
Pacific First Federal	$132.00
First State Bank	$80.00
Sears Roebuck Co.	$10.00
Home Lumber Co.	$20.00
Prematic [Insurance Co.]	$12.53
Telephone	$8.20
Electric	$13.47
Dimeo Oil Co.	$15.00
Prudential [Insurance Co.]	$41.75
[Montgomery] Wards	$10.00
Fred Meyer [Department Store]	$10.00
Meier and Frank [Department Store]	$5.00
Aloha Water	$6.75
Beaverton Auto	$8.50
Tualatin Valley Refuse	$5.25
Lerner's [Department Store]	$8.00
Catechism Supply Center	$3.70
Beginner Readers	$5.25
Lipman's [Department Store]	$12.00

February and March noted very similar entries, with the exception of an entry of $8.50 to Raleigh Hills Music Studio, $31.50 to Mom's Ob-Gyn, and $10.00 to our family doctor. In April there was an entry to our dentist for $75.00. Then I noticed a shift. Every month thereafter, additional doctors' names appeared, names like Cowger, Miller, Kreft, Hicks, Henton.... The list grew more extensive with each passing month. At one point I wrote up a list of all the doctors included in the ledger over the next two years and came up with a total of twenty-two additional names!

Juxtaposed alongside these mysterious (to me) doctors' expenses, seemingly normal life went right on, with entries to Miss Anita Pianove's School of Dance, Raleigh Hills Music Studio, and tuition payments to St. Mary's of the Valley School.

The more I studied this ledger, the more I realized it was telling the story of our family life. All these entries of Mom's many doctors reflect how troubled she was and how eager she was to get help, relief, and answers. And all the while Dad just kept putting one foot right in front of the other. Month after month, providing the (really big) little things for his kids: dance and music and quality education.

October 1965 lists the first of many subsequent entries for payments to Morningside Hospital. This would coincide with the documentation in Mom's medical records. These were the "hopscotching" periods between private treatment, home visits, and Dammasch State Hospital. This "game" eventually led to the unenviable "prize" of her being committed to Dammasch in August 1967.

As I continued to study the book of Dad's accounts, I flashed back in time as the story of our family during those years, listed in these expenses, unfolded with each turn of the page. Entries to Beaverton Ambulance Company reminded me of the horrible morning when Mom was whisked away after Rosie and I had slept out in our backyard.

When I saw the payments to Alpenrose Dairy, I swear I could almost taste the cold milk our milkman delivered weekly to a box on our front porch. And how Mom would skim the cream and sometimes make fresh butter or whip it into soft peaks to embellish her incredibly delectable cream puffs.

I read every page, both with the scrutiny of a crime detective following a trail of evidence and the heart of a child searching for her lost family. When I turned the page to June 1966, my heart nearly leapt from my chest. From June to September of that year were entries listing $2.00 each month to Father James Poole! Just seeing his name written in my father's handwriting was surreal and I was suddenly overcome by a wave of nausea. How could I have overlooked this before? Oh My God. This must be the Dollar-a-Month Club pledge Roseanne's attorney had mentioned!

But what really upset me was the timing of the entry. It was noted one year *after* Jim Poole had been transferred back to Alaska—a year in which Mom had been riding wave after wave of turbulent emotional confusion and mental torment. All the while during these stormy rides, my father had stood on the shore, trying in vain to save his wife from capsizing and drowning. No doubt he jumped into that crazy swirling ship a time or two along with her, still doing his best (though not always successfully) to keep us kids out of the path of the destructive winds. *What in the world were you thinking, Dad, when you wrote these $2.00 checks? Were you thinking?!*

I sat staring at the pages until the words began to blur. After a moment I closed the book, fearing that my tears might smear the tidy lists. I sat there for a long time and then reached for the phone to call Roseanne.

Chapter Seventeen
A RECORD OF PAIN, HEARTACHE, AND DIMINISHING HOPE

That humble book of my father's accounts became a key piece of evidence in the eventual settlement of Roseanne's case. Also instrumental were the medical records from our mother's time in Dammasch State Hospital, which documented her obsession with and guilt over her involvement with Jim Poole. The irony of acquiring these medical records was in how easy they were to obtain.

Roseanne had requested these of our Dad in the early '90s in hope of gaining a greater understanding of her mental illness, but Dad was adamant that these remain closed, claiming that he didn't think Mom would want us to see them. After much pleading and his continued refusal, Roseanne reluctantly let it go. What she didn't know at that time was that after twenty years these had become public records, and she could have obtained them without his permission. I guess we were just not meant to see them until the court subpoenaed them in April 2008.

In early May of that same year, so much evidence was in Roseanne's favor that the Church was finally ready to settle. I believe they wanted to avoid more public embarrassment if it did go to court.

I flew to Portland a few days before the hearing, specifically to spend time with Roseanne and Beth. With one another's mutual support, we would read through Mom's medical records together. I then planned to sit with Roseanne through her settlement hearing.

At best these were difficult enough to read with all the medical jargon, inconsistent forms, and mostly illegible handwritten clinic notes. About halfway through the middle of the first day of the gut-wrenching task of reading through the 450 disturbing and confusing pages, the box of records (thus far unnumbered, indexed, or correlated) fell onto the floor into a scrambled and even more chaotic mess.

With my nerves already on edge and my emotions in such turmoil, the upending of all those papers threatened to send me into a tailspin. I remember the sick feeling in my gut as I watched them scatter across the floor. What a picture of how we were all feeling that day, to see that scrambled mess of our mother's journey through mental illness spread out in such a crazy fashion on the floor.

I was so upset I had to step away from it and went out for a long walk. When I returned, Roseanne reported that she had called her attorney's assistant, Jen, who told us to come by her office and pick up a new set of copies. Being the competent person Jen is, she had this set numbered, indexed, and collated.

When we finally settled down once again to the task of reading these, the woman I called Mom and, whom I never really knew, began to be revealed from the pages of these documents. Both Roseanne and I were shocked by the many references to her violent outbursts and childish tantrums. We had never seen this side of our mother. I was heartbroken to read the harsh and clinical judgments of most of the doctors and aides who reported her progress. And I was equally touched by the kindness and compassion of a few aides who attended her and truly appeared to want to understand and help her.

As children, Rosie and I had glimpses into the darkness of her struggles, but (to Mom's credit) she managed, for the most part, to hide this side of herself, at least from her two youngest children. I suppose this might be why Dad didn't want us to read her records—his way of preserving our childhood memories of her.

As painful as it was, after reading these reports I feel I am better able to understand why my oldest sisters have such a hard time talking to us about that time. They were young adults and were not shielded in the same way as their "baby" sisters were.

As we read these notes and reports together, through the eyes of our personal experiences of that time, we each revisited that pain-filled period in our family's past with a mixture of shock, horror, sadness, and compassion.

Because Roseanne was currently studying to be a mental health counselor, and because she had worked in her ex-husband's psychiatric office, she was able to translate for us some of the medical jargon, including the drugs listed and some of their side effects; therefore, she was able, to some extent, to read with a degree of "academic" detachment. That is until we got to the page of daily progress notes dated October 27, 1967.

When we noted the timeline from when this was written, we realized that it corresponded with the dates when Rosie and I were first sent to live with the McDougall family. The following entry threatened to knock the emotional wind right out of us both:

October 27, 1967: Patient has horrible nightmares…. [one] dream is that her young children are crying for her.

When I read that aloud, Roseanne and I both broke down and wept. Two young children, now grown, once again crying for our mother, only this time we truly cried *for* her.

Chapter Eighteen
LET'S SETTLE THIS ONCE AND FOR ALL!

By late July and into early August 2008, the amount and type of evidence was so heavily stacked in Roseanne's favor that the Church's attorneys no doubt were beginning to sweat droplets as big as rosary beads. Following is what Roseanne said about it on August 12, 2008:

> The Jesuits started talking about bankruptcy. They knew that at trial, they could get slapped with $10–25 million in punitive damages in addition to whatever a jury would award me in personal injury damages.... And they also had had twenty new cases filed against other Jesuit priests in the last few months. Bankruptcy would be a sure way that my case would never go to trial. This was their only line of defense and the only card they could play. It was a devastating blow. We expected the defense to simply cancel the mediation and file, but curiously they didn't.
>
> A big financial reward was enticing, but I was keeping my expectations very low. After all, any amount would be more than what I started this process with. So when we got to the mediation yesterday morning, we really expected that they were going to offer something so low that it would be more beneficial for me to go through the bankruptcy process, because I would "probably" (more lawyer optimism) get a fairly decent award out of that, but the process would drag on for a couple more years. I was ready to just call it a day, forget about it, and tell the lawyers to call me in a couple of years when something actually happened.

The mediation hearing was not canceled. Early in the morning of Monday, August 11, Roseanne crawled alongside me in the guest bed I was sleeping in at her house. Together we prayed for God's will and for the grace to accept the outcome of the day's proceedings. We both had a strong sense that this was *the day.*

The next most important piece of business we sisters had to address was what does one wear to such an event? I was especially pleased with Roseanne's choice: a short, formfitting, lime green shift with big white polka dots, which she referred to as her happy dress.

I accompanied Roseanne to one of downtown Portland's many office buildings within a vast high rise complex, where we met with her pack of lawyers. The proceedings were scheduled to begin at 9:00 AM. The building itself was awe inspiring for a little ol' Montana girl like me, with multiple stories of reflective glass windows that towered above the city. Of particular fascination to me was how many of the internal offices were also made of glass walls, creating openness to the whole interior. During breaks, we would walk around to stretch our legs, and we could even see into the room down the hall where the defendant's lawyers were conferring with their clients.

The process was fascinating. The mediator, a spitfire attorney with a dripping Texas drawl, reigned supreme in her role. Though diminutive in physical stature, her titan presence filled the room. Her obvious intelligence combined with her many years of experience lent an air of unquestionable confidence. Juxtaposed to these qualities, an outrageous witty sense of humor and the resultant banter with the other "players" in the room lent levity to the process that helped us all to (almost) feel relaxed.

As I sat next to Roseanne at the large table, across from what she referred to as her dream team of defense attorneys, I felt a sense of being a fly on the wall as history was in the making. In Roseanne's words:

> The events of yesterday will forever be imprinted on my mind. The process was amazing to watch. These really were some of the most knowledgeable and skilled lawyers in the country who were assembled in this conference room on my behalf. From early on, this case has taken on a life of its own, and in many ways it did not feel like it was even about me, and it was somewhat surreal to be sitting there in a room with these guys.
>
> From the beginning of this entire process, I found all of them [Roseanne's lawyers and their aides] to be men and women of principle and integrity. Never once did I feel any

sense of being used, deceived, scammed, or swindled like I feared [might happen]. I also learned that they had genuine compassion and a devoted sense of responsibility to their clients.

[I was encouraged to] try to get the most I could out of them [the defendant] today and get them to guarantee that they wouldn't file bankruptcy for ninety days (else my settlement would be reversed by the bankruptcy court).

In the end I was awarded [an amount] about twice as much as anyone had hoped for at the beginning of the day. I could have never imagined such a thing. And I am still in shock.

What is important for me to say in the end of this process is that I somewhat cringe when someone comments that I deserve it.

However, what I will say is that they, the Catholic Church, the Jesuits deserve it. They deserve to be held accountable for their horrendous history of turning a blind eye to abuse of thousands of children and adults by the priests who were supposed to be trustworthy ministers of God's love. The damage done by the abusing priests themselves has been abhorrent. But the actions of the Church leaders and hierarchy who proceeded to cover it up and move the priest to new locations without any protection for new victims is [*sic*] truly evil.

I want to thank all of my family for supporting me and at least tolerating the process. I am very relieved that there won't be any public trial, and no one will have to be further interrogated or asked to testify. I have gathered a lot of material throughout this process, which shed a great deal of light on what happened to our mother and how Father Poole's encounter with our family forever changed the trajectory of all of [our] lives.

Now I am looking for closure. Therefore, for my sake and the sake of anyone of you who wants to join me, I have also negotiated as part of my settlement to have a family meeting with the Provincial in charge of the Jesuits and Father Poole, who is eighty-two years old, is of very sound mind and body, and [is currently living in a private retirement home in Spokane, Washington]. Though he never admitted to ever knowing anyone in our family, even when shown photos, he was clearly able to remember everything else about the time he was in Portland. It is my intention to take this opportunity to let him know the sequel to the story of the Mueller family, whom he quickly disregarded once he returned to Alaska. The sequel is the damage he caused me, the destruction he set in motion for our mother, the pain he caused our father, and eventually the pain he caused all of us.

Chapter Nineteen
BACK AT THE TABLE
JUST DESSERTS, PLEASE

Forgiveness is not an event where you utter pious words that somehow release the accused and yourself as well. It is not denying the wrong ever occurred. It is not forgetting the events of your past ever took place. It is not a spiritual way of saying that the wrong done to you is all right and of no consequence. It is not self-martyrdom. It is not cheap, quick, or easy. It is not automatically trusting or even liking the person who hurt you. These are all things that forgiveness is not. Now let's talk about what it is.

In the Hebrew, which is a picture language, the word forgiveness looks like this: To burn. To carry away. To bear or endure. To pardon from penalty. To suffer. (Ouch!) To lift off the weight of burden. In Greek: To forsake. To lay aside. To put away. To yield up. To sustain damage. To send away from me.

Forgiveness is to lift off the weight of the debt, to send it away, and to absorb or suffer the damage myself. Forgiveness is a process, not an event. It takes time for a "process" to process. Healing and forgiveness both take time.

While forgiveness removes the poison of resentment from your body, grace completely neutralizes the toxin so that no one can ever be harmed by it again.[1]

January 2009

The mornings' snowstorm had finally subsided, and a momentary sparkle of reflected light bounced off the Willamette River. As I stared out the expansive window of Roseanne's attorney's conference room window, my attention was once again drawn to the imposing view of the Freemont Bridge.

Then, just as suddenly as it had a made its appearance, a gray cloud moved across the sky, obscuring the sun. I felt an involuntary chill as my attention was brought fully back into the room.

Roseanne sat across the table from the two priests. Having made her introductions, she had begun to read from the notes she had composed prior to this meeting, first addressing Jim Poole regarding his supposed memory loss of his involvement with our family.

My heart swelled with pride for her as she read. The clarity and composure of her thoughts and words filled the room with a calm sense of authoritative grace.

Turning her attention away from Jim Poole, she now addressed the second of the two men seated across from her. "My second purpose is to speak to Father Lee and ask him to use his leadership position in the Jesuit Order to finally take a stand against the cover-ups and lies that have been the characteristic response by the Church and the Pope himself to claims of abuse."

Then turning back to Jim Poole, she continued. "Mr. Poole, you reached out to my mother when in the course of caring for her son, [and] she became involved with you through Jesuit High School, where you were sent in 1965 under the guise of a cover story [that was written at the time of your transfer]: that you were sent there to raise funds for the St. Mary's Mission in Alaska. [See Appendix C.] Even Rome had been consulted on the problems you were causing at St. Mary's, and their response was to send you into another ministry without any restrictions on your interactions with female parishioners and children. Thus you befriended my mother and lured her into a romantic relationship. At the same time you took the opportunity to sexually molest me and groom me for being molested by another Jesuit priest, Frank Duffy.

"When you met my mother, Martha Mueller, she was a troubled woman. But she had spent her life in faithful devotion to God and to the Catholic Church. She sent her children to Catholic schools, attended Mass, and tithed to the Church faithfully. She personally taught us about God and prayer and to have compassion on the poor and downtrodden. When she needed loving support and counsel from the Church, she was instead deceived and exploited by you.

"After you left and returned to Alaska, she never recovered her dignity. She was tormented by guilt for what she was made to believe was her own sin. She sought help and absolution from numerous other priests, one of whom was Frank Duffy. Her connection with Frank Duffy gave him access to me. He took that opportunity to rape me, and he terrified me and set my life on a path of shame and self-doubt.

"According to Martha's medical records and other accounts from people who knew her well, she wrote you many letters and remained preoccupied for the rest of her life with making sense of what happened between you and her. After numerous attempts she eventually committed suicide on April 11, 1971, the eve of Easter Sunday.

"That day I believe that God received her in His loving arms. Amazingly, she also believed in a loving, forgiving God, even though the Church taught that suicide was a [mortal] sin. I am so grateful to know that she died with the hope and knowledge of salvation and not condemnation."

For a moment Roseanne was silent. And as she set down her notes, she looked Jim Poole squarely in the face. She picked up a sheet of paper from a small pile before her and went on. "I would [now] like to read you [a portion of] her suicide note."

Roseanne, Beth, and I had already read this, having acquired it from the Clackamas County Authorities shortly after reading through Mom's medical records. However, our brother, C.J., had not yet read it, though we had mentioned it to him to prepare him for its content. Now as Roseanne began to read our mother's final words, I glanced over, hoping to gauge his response.

"*'When will anyone ever believe I am not wicked and evil, but insane with longing to feel loved by God and man?'*"

As Roseanne recited our mother's desperate plea for understanding, C.J. sat listening, stoically silent as she finished reading Mom's words.

"*'I am insane and I am going to try to take my life tonight so I can feel loved by God, and God will make me forget that I ever hated Him for not taking my life himself.'*"

A palpable heaviness settled over the room as Roseanne set the paper containing Mom's final words on the table before her. She glanced briefly at C.J., and I saw them exchange a look of deep sorrow. He appeared to me to be making a valiant attempt to hold his emotions in check.

Then Roseanne resumed her address to the men seated across from her.

"What you did to me was damaging, and it affected my life in many ways. But what you did to our mother you also did to me and to my entire family, not just our generation but to our children and their children. Mary and I had very sad and lonely childhoods, and we did not have the benefit of a mother to teach us about life and to teach us how to be mothers ourselves. All of Martha's children suffered in different ways because of this. Our father, Clarence, suffered in ways we will never fully know."

She paused briefly to look up when the door opened and our brother slipped quietly out of the room. As she resumed her reading, I followed C.J., moments behind, in search of where he might have gone. When I peeked into the small staff kitchen/break room down the hall, I found him in a corner, leaning with his forehead pressed against the wall above the microwave oven, his shoulders shaking in heaving sobs.

"Hey, Bro, you gonna be okay?" I whispered.

He kept his face to the wall as I placed my hands gently onto the tops of his shoulders and began a soft massaging motion.

"Yeah, I just find this so hard. Seeing him again and being reminded of what he did to all of us."

I had a sudden sick feeling in my gut as a thought that surprisingly had not occurred to me until this moment came to my mind. Haltingly I put my thoughts into the air.

"Did he molest you too, C.J.?" I held my breath, hoping for a negative response.

He turned his tear-streaked face up from the wall, and I felt my breath release in a sigh of relief at his reply.

"No, he did not." He shook his head and gave an exasperated sigh. "But what Roseanne said was right on: what he did to Mom and Roseanne he also did to our entire family."

"You got that right, brother." I pulled him into an embrace. I had not ever witnessed my adult brother weep, and now for the second time today, I felt my heart would break for him as we held each other in the corner of that little room.

After a few moments I stepped back and waited for him to look up.

"Just give me a few minutes to get myself together, okay?"

"All right." I patted his back. "I love you."

"Back atcha." He nodded as I left the room.

When I slipped back into the conference room, Roseanne glanced up at me with an imploring look that I knew was one of concern for our brother. I nodded in response and mouthed, "He's okay" and wiped an invisible tear from my eye as a silent signal.

Before referring back to her notes she gave a wan smile, sadly shaking her head. She continued to read from the papers before her.

"Lastly, I would like to say that I have a dear aunt and uncle who have been faithful, devoted servants to the Church here in the Portland area for over sixty years. They sent every one of their eight children through St. Mary's, St. Cecilia's, and Jesuit High School. They have surely tithed their income and most definitely their hearts faithfully for all those years. It grieves me to know that because of the Church's unwillingness to honestly repent and remove these priests from active ministry and from the priesthood altogether, that the tithes of faithful servants like my aunt and uncle are being squandered on lawyers and the endless effort to save face by covering the truth of what the Church is clearly guilty of.

"Severe action against these priests and new policies in place to protect children in the future are what the victims want more than financial compensation from the Church. Unfortunately, the only thing we can see to do is to continue to [apply] financial pressure until the pain of it causes repentance and, most important, reform."

She then gathered her papers and tapped them on end onto the table, straightening them into a neat pile. Placing them firmly onto the spot in front of her, she let out her breath and closed her eyes briefly as though to say, "I am finished." (For Roseanne's full message to the priests, see Appendix D.)

Father Lee looked across the table at her and began to lift his hand as though he were a student asking permission to speak.

"I understand you may be feeling the need to respond to my words, and I will give you that opportunity when we are finished here. However, my sister Beth has something she would like to say, and so if you will, please leave your comments until we are done." Roseanne then turned her attention toward Beth as she shifted in her seat, deliberately dismissing the priests.

All eyes turned to Beth, seated at the far end of the large table as she picked up her sheaf of notes and began to read from them.

"Mr. Poole," she began, a bit nervously at first.

"My name is Elizabeth Mueller-Price. My mother was Martha Mueller." Her voice gained confidence and authority. "She was a lovely woman with five girls and one boy and a husband who was completely devoted to her. Martha fully embraced God and the Catholic Church. She believed, as she was taught, that the priests were God's representatives on earth.

"She raised all six children to revere and hold sacred the Church and the priests. When you, Mr. Poole, came into our family circle, it was with wicked, criminal intent. You may not see it that way, but a court of law has proven it true. You were the catalyst that tore our family apart. Your relationship with our mother took her to the brink of a living hell. I hold you responsible for our mother's death. All she ever believed about the sanctity of the Church was destroyed. She could not face her pain any longer. She took her life.

"My two younger sisters, Mary and Roseanne, were sixteen and thirteen years old [respectively]. They were left motherless. They had to bare the shame of suicide, after all, it was [taught that it was] a mortal sin. Roseanne had to keep secrets of your abuse buried in her heart for forty years. I know my brother was affected, but, to this day, he cannot talk about it."

She stopped reading just long enough to look across the room at each of her siblings seated at the table. We exchanged a brief knowing look of agreement before she continued. Narrowing her eyes slightly, she then peered at Jim Poole, who sat staring straight ahead, as though into some great expanse before him. His rhythmic thumb twirling hesitated for the briefest of moments.

"My life spun out of control. My heart was crushed. My emotions went numb. Tragic, regretful events took place in my life. Some of the outcome was due to your counsel to my mother. Our two oldest sisters, Joan and Diana, had to be affected, but they do not feel comfortable to this day in sharing their thoughts with me."

Softening her tone, she continued, "I believe you and I are the same in our humanity." We came into this world with original sin. The difference between us is this: when God came into my life in

1972, I repented of my sins and I gave my life to Him. You, Mr. Poole," she said, raising her voice with an air of authority and pointing to the papers in her hands at him, "have not repented of your sins."

Then again her voice softened. "I cannot be your judge. God will be your judge. You will stand before Him soon. You will have to answer for every word, thought, and deed committed in your life."

She went on to share with him a parable of Jesus found in the book of Matthew, chapter 13. This parable begins in verse 3 with a man sowing seed, and ends in verses 41–43 with Jesus's explanation of the parable concerning his judgment of both good and evil.

When she finished reading this compelling parable, she looked up and addressed him once more, her voice an appeal.

"There will be a day of reckoning for you, Mr. Poole. Where will you be? If you don't know, the answer is not hidden."

At this point she hesitated for a few moments, and I became acutely aware of the clock ticking on the south wall. It seemed to me as though the sound of the ticking clock intensified in the otherwise silent room. Tic, toc, tic, toc, it echoed into the momentary stillness.

Beth then reached for a small pamphlet on the table before her. She slid this across the table to Jim. Reluctantly, he picked it up and began to glance through it.

"What you are holding is a written message that I would like to share with you. This was the teaching that was given to me when I first came to know the Lord. It is called the Four Spiritual Laws."[2]

Jim Poole squirmed ever so slightly as she asked him to follow along with her while she explained it to him. I have no doubt that it galled him to be given a religious lesson, as though he were the student in a catechism class rather than the priest. I'm sure he saw himself as the true authority.

So she gave a religious lesson regarding God's grace and forgiveness to the man whom she had just moments ago accused of visiting horrendous devastation in all of our lives, not to mention the utter ruin of our mother.

I am ashamed to admit that I felt a sense of appalling disbelief that she would even think of this. But didn't Jesus tell us to—

gulp—love our enemies, to pray for those who persecute us? I watched in fascination as my amazingly gracious sister carried out that very command before all of our eyes.

At one point in her "lesson," there was a word picture that none of us that day had any way of knowing just how profoundly God would use to illustrate a key point.

Beth was describing, in the words of the pamphlet, how great the gulf is between God and man. She instructed Father Poole to turn and look out the window and then asked him, "What do you see?"

It was in that moment that the Freemont Bridge once again came clearly into focus, as though one might step onto it and cross over to the other side.

"Well, obviously, a bridge," Jim said.

"Yes, it's a bridge!" Beth then told him to refer to the page open before him. There in picture form was the illustration of Jesus as the Bridge of God's Grace. (To read Beth's full message, see Appendix E.)

I suddenly flashed back in my own memory to a day nearly forty years prior, when I sat at another table with Beth. I was a young teenage mother, depressed, motherless, and feeling so very lost. She used this same pamphlet to explain to me how much God loved me and held out the promise of hope that He had a wonderful plan for my life. "Where are you going, Mary?" she had asked.

I had no other answer but, "Nowhere."

That was the day I chose to hand over the direction of my life to the Lord. Beth had also shared this same message with Roseanne around that same time, to which Roseanne responded, as did I, with a prayer of surrender.

And now here we were, the "Three God Sisters", sitting together in this room while Beth held out the same message of grace and salvation to the most unlikely (and might I add, most undeserving) person in the most inconceivable circumstances.

I wish I could tell you that he fell to his knees in repentant sorrow, but, sadly, he did not—at least not that day, in that room, not that any of us witnessed. He stubbornly held to his resolute defense of "failed memory." Most likely, none of us will ever know, at least in this lifetime, if he ever will admit to any of his many crimes. What I do know is that by our act of forgiving him, *we* have been set free. As for Jim Poole, as Beth stated, only God can judge.

Each person will one day cross over the bridge from this life to the other side. And when they do, He will be waiting. And in His hands will be a book, a book of accounts. He alone holds the final book of accounts: my (Heavenly) Father's Ledger.

Afterword
THE GREATEST LOVE OF ALL

Where is Love?

Where is love? Does it fall from skies above?
Is it underneath the willow tree that I've been dreaming of?
Where is she? Whom I close my eyes to see?
Will I ever know the sweet hello that's meant for only me?
Who can say where she may hide? Must I travel far and wide?
'Til I am beside the someone who I can mean something to?
Where, oh where, is love?

Lionel Bart, *Oliver!*

March 2013

First Corinthians 13, known commonly as the Love Chapter, is the ideal example of what perfect love looks like: patient, kind, longsuffering. Verses 4–8 are a beautiful recitation of the many qualities we all aspire to but none of us can possibly maintain all the time. We're only human, so we keep trying when we miss the mark and hope to learn to love more perfectly as we grow in maturity, right?

The chapter closes with verse 13: "So now faith, hope and love abide, these three; but the greatest of these is love" (ESV). But tucked into the middle of all this lofty idealism is verse 11: "When I was a child, I spoke like a child, I thought like a child, I reasoned like a child. When I became a man [woman], I gave up my childish ways."

Was Oliver's cry merely a wish-filled dream, hoping that he would someday find out, "Where, oh where, is love?" Did he know what he was asking in his childish song? Where is love, indeed?

Well, I'm thinking maybe that's the same quest my mother was on her whole life. She was dreaming underneath a "willow tree" of childhood pain and neglect, waiting for it to "fall from skies above." And, yes, she did travel far and wide looking for "someone whom she could mean something to."

The unfortunate news about her travels is that she journeyed to places she never intended to go. And the greatest misfortune of all was her final destination, the place none who knew and loved her ever wanted her to go. Sadly, she was led by travel guides who turned out to be some of the most unscrupulous she could have hooked up with.

Though many good and well-meaning folks tried to help her find her way to where love is, she never could seem to find it. The big It: love.

I was mulling over this idea of love, God's love, one day not long ago when He reminded me of just how great is His love for me, for all of His children. And this message came to me in the most unusual manner, in the most unlikely of places.

I was standing in the housewares aisle of Target, looking for some shelving for my office. Though I was there physically, my mind was elsewhere. Having recently been through a difficult period with one of my adult children, my emotions were in turmoil and very close to the surface of my fragile self-composure.

This recent situation was weighing so heavily on my heart. I was truly in need of a dose of what I call Daddy-God Love. You know the feeling that you just want to climb up into His big ol' lap and have a good cry while He rocks you off to sleep—that kind of love.

As I was sorting through the selection of shelving, from somewhere over my left shoulder I heard the sweetest woman's voice singing. "Jesus loves me this I know for the bible tells me so… Yes, Jesus loves me! Yes, Jesus loves me! Yes, Jesus loves me. The Bible tells me so."

And then the music faded. I looked to see from where this lovely melody was coming. And I realized it was coming from one of those music sample kiosks, a large box-like poster where you push the button to hear a few lines from the featured CD selections. The odd thing was that no one was standing near it, and this had headphones you had to wear to hear the selection.

I can hardly begin to describe how this affected me. Instantly I was struck by how incongruous it was, to hear "Jesus Loves Me" broadcast aloud while standing in the housewares of Target. But there it was, and in the sweetest, singsong lullaby voice.

No one else was around, so I knew it was a special message just for me. The emotions that a few moments ago were at the back of my subconscious were now tears streaming down my face. Still looking around, I saw no one as I walked to the restroom to gather my composure.

Yes, *Jesus loves me! Yes, Jesus loves me!* echoed across the canyon of my wide-open heart as I sat in the bathroom stall, trying to catch my breath. This was not a song I learned as a child growing up in a Catholic home. This was not a song I learned at St. Mary's of the Valley Academy for Young Girls or from a hymnal stuck in the pew of St. Cecilia's Church.

It's more of a Protestant hymn, I think, but the truth is I felt It—God's love—all my life. I felt It when I saw the crucifix that hung over the altar as the priest performed the sacraments. I felt It whenever I dipped my finger in a holy-water fount and genuflected. I felt It whenever we gathered in our living room to say the Rosary, when my father lit the candles and dimmed the lights and led us in the hypnotic, repetitious prayers. When I looked around the room and saw my family all there with their heads bowed and my mother looking enraptured in the candlelight, I felt *It*.

In preparing to write this story, I have learned a lot about my mother and her lifelong quest to feel It—God's love for her—which is amazing to me, because in my eyes she extended godly love for others in so many ways. But I have the distinct advantage of viewing her with the eyes of a child. If you can call it an advantage, at least one "benefit" of losing your mother when you are young is that she is held in child-like memory, without the baggage collected in relationships during those difficult teen and young adult years.

Although she died when I was sixteen, in actuality she went away when I was about ten. The imposter that claimed to be my mother still went by the same name as my mother. I will now refer to her as my Magical Mother. Let's just call her MM for short, which ironically were her initials. Magical because she developed the uncanny ability to disappear. Then she could—*poof!*—reappear again.

Every time she did this amazing magic trick, I noticed that my Real Mother, the one I had always known to be strong and kind and patient, was becoming a stranger to me, to all of us. The woman who slipped in little by little as she began to disappear more and more was a mystery. Maybe MM could also stand for Mystery Mother.

From my point of view, my mother, my Real Mother, was a loving and godly woman who modeled grace and compassion in so many ways. Like when she insisted on taking in borders for the holiday season from St. Mary's Home for Boys. One summer she invited fourteen-year-old twin brothers, Ronald and Roland, to go on a camping trip with us. They were the first black people I'd ever talked to or spent any time with in my very sheltered Caucasian, middle-class, suburban upbringing. She treated them like they were just regular people (which, of course, they were) and taught me not to judge others by the color of their skin. I felt It whenever we drove into the big city of Portland, when upon seeing homeless people she'd say, "But for the grace of God, there go I." Again, don't judge. I'd see It when I heard her say, "If you can't say something nice, don't say anything at all."

That she was never able to fully grasp the magnitude of God's love for herself is the overarching tragedy of this story, and I believe the key to the dark spell this MM must have held over her.

If I were by some great miracle of God able to go back in time to spend even five minutes with her, to be able to impart a word of truth—one she could truly grasp and take into her soul, a word that could have changed everything—I would share with her one of the most profound theological truths I have ever come across. This is It:

Jesus loves me! This I know,
For the Bible tells me so;
Little ones to Him belong;
They are weak, but He is Strong.

Yes, Jesus loves me!
Yes, Jesus loves me!
Yes, Jesus loves. The Bible tells me so.

Anna B. Warner

"For this reason I kneel before the Father, from whom His whole family derives its name. I pray that out of His glorious riches He may strengthen you with power through His Spirit in your inner being, so that Christ may dwell in your hearts through faith.

"And I pray that you, being rooted and established in love, may have power, together with all the Lord's holy people, to grasp how wide and long and high and deep is the love of Christ, and to know this love that surpasses knowledge—that you may be filled to the measure of all the fullness of God.

*"Now to Him who is able to do immeasurably more than we all we ask and imagine, according to His power that is at work within us, to Him be glory in the church and in Christ Jesus **through all generations,** for ever and ever! Amen."*

Ephesians 3:14–21 NIV, emphasis mine.

Appendix A
UNDERSTANDING THE PREDATOR-VICTIM DYNAMIC

I n the process of studying about Mom's life, I have obtained a much deeper understanding of her progression into mental illness. As for her and Roseanne's victimization of sexual abuse, I have also gained a greater insight.

By way of summary I will touch on a few of the highlights (or perhaps I should call them low points) of what I have learned. These are my own personal, subjective opinions and are by no means meant to be a professional evaluation.

Mom was born in 1924 into a large, very poor, old-school (read: guilt, shame) Catholic family. At the time of her birth, her mother was suffering from severe depression following the loss of her oldest son in a drowning accident. Mom's care was largely left to her older siblings, who greatly resented having this task put on them. Her father, whom she described as a serious, distant figure in the family, was preoccupied with supporting his large family during the difficult years of the Great Depression of the late 1920s and '30s.

Thus Mom never experienced a healthy, secure attachment with either of her parents. Her older siblings referred to her as a "whiny brat." When my father discussed with her father his desire to marry her, he was warned that she was a "cry baby."

As a young adolescent, Mom was subjected to sexual abuse by an older male family member. When she reported this to her mother, she was chastised for lying, thus adding more fuel to the fiery shame of this violation.

Add up all of these factors: poverty, neglect, sexual abuse, religious oppression—with an emphasis on guilt, shame, and fear—and your chances for a healthy, secure sense of self are pretty low.

However, in spite of all these disadvantages, as an adult she did the best she could (remarkably so) to overcome and make a better life for herself and her family. She wanted to give us kids all the things she lacked in her own young life: cleanliness, education, financial security, stability, and the greatest of these—love.

The unfortunate thing is how very important the outward appearances of being a good wife and mother and the (sadly unmet) expectation of the hoped for feelings of fulfillment as a woman. All of these factors were directly tied to her personal sense of worth.

Her inability to control the normal independent, rebellious behavior of her maturing children became an increasingly frustrating problem for her that she further translated as a personal failure.

Also of great importance to her was the achievement of acquiring the beautiful new home with the house full of shiny new furnishings, as well as the crown jewel of a professionally landscaped yard.

She and my father had worked hard for many years before they realized this great American Dream. The big move into the new house took place in 1963, around the time her chronic depression had begun to consume her. The irony of this achievement, the other side of this golden coin, was the utter disappointment that even this did not fill the longing in her heart. Perhaps she believed that the new house and all the furnishings would be the key to her happiness. But once she had obtained it and it did not satisfy, what else was there?

Then there is Roseanne. She was born in 1958, just prior to the real onset of Mom's hormonal and emotional upheaval. The last child of six, she spent most of her days home alone with Mom as a small child, while we older kids were in school. She has shared with me that her earliest memories of being with Mom were of feeling "in the way" and that she made a concerted effort not to upset her, walking around on emotional eggshells. She experienced a deep sense of concern over Mom's unhappiness, believing somehow that it was her fault. She also expressed feeling "lost and alone" much of the time. This sense of loneliness most certainly set her up for being vulnerable to the attention of a skilled child predator.

Enter the priests, the men whom Mom most admired and looked up to at the time of her greatest need and seven-year-old Roseanne was taught to believe in as an agent of God, and you have the perfect setup for a dual victim-predator relationship.

Predators seek out and prey on those who are insecure, weak, and vulnerable—those who do not have a strong enough sense of self-assurance to say no, to fight back, to know that their caregivers will protect and validate them. For many, their primary caregivers may also be their abusers.

In addition, confusion in the mind of children as to who exactly are the adults who are supposed to protect them further muddles their thinking. And when abusers tell the children that they are bad if they don't do what the abusers want and that they are really bad if they tell anyone about the abuse, the victims become even more bewildered and take on unwarranted guilt.

I believe these are some of the key components for both Mom and Roseanne that set them up to be exploited, used, and abused by the predator-priests in this all too true story.

If you have been a victim of childhood (or adult) sexual abuse, you may be able to relate to many aspects of this story. I hope I have turned on a light of understanding for you. But you may be thinking, "That's all very well and good, but, you know, it's been a lot of years, and what good is that information to me now? The damage has been done and I can't go back and undo any of it." The truth is none of us can go back and change our pasts.

However, a new understanding can change the way we view it. And we can, by the grace of God, along with the resources available to us, heal from the damage caused by our past experiences.

You may be struggling with some of the mental/emotional health issues I brought up in this story, i.e., depression, sexual abuse; past or present, suicidal thoughts and/or attempts. Or perhaps you have a loved one suffering with these issues, or you may be a survivor of a loved one lost to suicide. I encourage you to seek out reliable, professional help.

Help and healing may come in the form of counseling with a therapist trained to specifically address your particular issue(s). You can find books, videos, audio tapes, and numerous support groups that can help as well. A combination of all of these could be most helpful. I pray you do all you can to bring these resources into your life.

There is hope. You are loved. You can heal. Life can be good. You are worth it!

Appendix B
PAPAL SECRETS POLICY

Excerpts from the case of Jane Doe 2, Alaska, pages 43–45

F ather Thomas Doyle, an expert on Church administration and canon law, testified that in 1962, the Vatican published a special set of rules regarding clergy sexual malfeasance, which remained in effect until 2001. These rules (the "pontifical" secret or the "papal secret") required total secrecy by the Church and its lay members regarding any allegations of sexual abuse by a priest. Even the rules themselves were required to be kept secret. A Church member found to have violated the policy was subject to excommunication from the Church....

...When the Church had a policy, set by the Pope and punishable by excommunication, not to reveal anything about sexual abuse by priests, the presiding Bishop's reaction to any concern was to exercise spin control and *not admit anything,* and only Church officials knew about the prior concerns about Poole. (Emphasis mine.)

Appendix C
SUMMARY JUDGMENT

["Papal Secrets" and the "Cover Story"]

Excerpts from the Opposition to Defendant's Motion for Summary Judgment on the Statute of Limitations, June 14, 2008, pages 3–6.

After years of internal and external warnings to the Jesuits about the bizarre sexual conduct of Father James Poole around children, especially girls, including warnings from nuns, priests, and even intervention from the top Jesuit in Rome, Defendant [The Society of Jesus, Oregon Province], in 1964 , decided to move Poole from Alaska to Portland. There it was reasoned, Poole could be at an *all-boys* school... where, ostensibly, he might straighten up. (Emphasis mine.)

Of course, transferring such a high-profile priest as Father Poole might create even more scandal. So the Defendant invented a "cover-story"—Defendant's words—that Poole was in Portland "to raise money for the Alaska missions." Such a representation was manifestly and knowingly false. However, by placing Poole in Portland and presenting him to the Jesuit and Catholic community as a priest in good standing, Defendant essentially certified Poole as in compliance with the rigorous moral standard of a Catholic priest, including most centrally that he was celibate.

Plaintiff's [Roseanne] family bought into the misrepresentation. Her mother, a sad depressive, who [ultimately] committed suicide when Plaintiff was 13, in her problems revered and idolized Poole, and Plaintiff saw that. Poole apparently provided pastoral counseling to Plaintiff's mother, and Plaintiff observed that.

He [Poole] arranged for Plaintiff's sister—unexpectedly and embarrassingly pregnant [at age eighteen]—to go to a home for unwed mothers. In this role, Poole was a frequent visitor in the home. For all these reason, Plaintiff trusted and revered Poole, who built what seemed to the seven-year-old to be a simple friendship. Then he abused her. Likewise with Father Duffy, Defendant had years of trouble with his sexual acting out....

...Thus, despite numerous notices to Defendant that Father Duffy was not sexually safe, he was assigned to Jesuit High School in Portland, where Plaintiff's family came to know him. Duffy abused Plaintiff on numerous occasions over a period of several years. Ironically and poignantly, one of these incidents occurred while Plaintiff's mother was out of the home in a pastoral counseling session with Father Poole, and Father Duffy was babysitting the Plaintiff to help facilitate Poole's time with the Plaintiff's mother.

Appendix D
ROSEANNE'S STATEMENT TO THE PRIESTS

I would like to begin today by saying that I don't have any expectations for either of you to make any kind of statement or apology to me. In fact, I would almost prefer that you didn't try to say anything to appease me. I would also like to say that I prefer not to refer to you as "Father" Poole, I will refer to you as Mr. Poole.

That said, I will introduce myself. I am Roseanne Miller. My maiden name was Mueller. My mother was Martha Mueller, a woman who you befriended in 1965 when you came to Oregon. My father was Clarence Mueller.

I have two reasons for requesting this meeting today: The first is to remind you, Mr. Poole, since you claim to have forgotten, about my family and your involvement with us. I want to let you know the sequel of what happened in our lives after you went back to Alaska and carried on you work of damaging the lives of countless other women and children.

The second purpose is to speak to Father Lee and ask him to use his leadership position in the Jesuit order to finally take a stand against the cover-ups and lies that have been the characteristic response by the Church and the Pope himself to the claims of abuse.

Mr. Poole, you reached out to my mother when in the course of caring for her son, my brother, [and] she became involved with you through Jesuit High School, where you were sent in 1965 under the guise of a "cover story" that you were sent there to fund-raise money for the St. Mary's mission in Alaska. Even Rome had been consulted on the problems you were causing at St. Mary's and their response was to send you into another ministry without any restrictions on your interactions with female parishioners and children. Thus you befriended my mother and lured her into a romantic relationship. At the same time, you took the opportunity to sexually molest me and groom me for being molested by another Jesuit priest, Frank Duffy.

When you met my mother, Martha Mueller, she was a troubled woman. But she had spent her life in faithful devotion to God and the Catholic Church. She sent her children to Catholic schools, attended Mass, and tithed to the church faithfully. She personally taught us about God and prayer and to have compassion on the poor and downtrodden. When she needed loving support and counsel from the church, she was instead deceived and exploited by you. After you left and returned to Alaska, she never recovered her dignity. She was tormented by guilt for what she was made to believe was her own sin. She sought help and absolution from numerous other priests, one of whom was Frank Duffy. Her connection with Frank Duffy gave him access to me. He took that opportunity to rape me and he terrified me and set my life on a path of shame and self-doubt. According to Martha's medical records and other accounts from people who knew her well, she wrote you many letters and remained preoccupied with making sense of what had happened between you and her for the rest of her life. (After numerous attempts she eventually committed suicide on April 11, 1971, the eve of Easter Sunday.)

That day, I believe that God received her in His loving arms. Amazingly, she also believed in a loving forgiving God, even though the Church taught that suicide was a sin. I am so grateful to know that she died with the hope and knowledge of salvation and not condemnation.

What you did to me was damaging and it affected my life in many ways. But what you did to our mother you also did to me and to my entire family, not just our generation, but to our children and their children. Mary and I had very sad and lonely childhoods, and we did not have the benefit of a mother to teach us about life and to teach us how to be mothers ourselves. All of Martha's children suffered in different ways because of this. Our father, Clarence, suffered in ways that we will never fully know.

I am aware that there were many other women and children who you exploited in some way. I have heard and read their stories. This is between you and God. But I would offer a suggestion that you finally abandon your collusion with the Catholic Church to deny and cover up these sins, and risk being ostracized by the church in order for you to publicly confess your sins and expose the truth for the sake of your victims and their families, who deserve to be validated and reach closure. You should do this for your own sake as well, so that when you stand before God, you can stand on the truth of your own repentance and not the false absolution of another priest, a mere human being no greater that you who has no power to forgive sins. Only true remorse toward your fellow man and true confession before God will suffice to cleanse your heart from sin.

To Father Lee, I would like to say that I speak for myself and I believe for many other victims and their families when I say that we are sick of hearing the sanitized, self-protective and dishonest media responses the Church around the world has made regarding this insidious problem within your organization. We are sickened and wounded again and again by your choice to protect the priests that have perpetrated sexual crimes against the parishioners who trusted you with their children and their very faith in a loving God. You must once and for all stop protecting yourselves and especially harboring and coddling these abusive priests. You must stop fighting against the lawsuits that are brought and seek to settle them honestly and quickly.

I can tell you honestly that if I had read in the newspaper that the Jesuits and the Roman Catholic Church has admitted that they were wrong when they did not take stricter action against Poole and other priests like him, in the '60 s, '70's, and '80 s, and admitted to knowingly moving him into other ministries when he caused damage to children, I would not have filed my case. I believe that this would have been true for hundreds of others who also filed cases. I am convinced that if you [had] asked those who have brought cases against the Church, many would say that they are angrier at the Church's response than they are at the priest who abused them. This is a travesty of justice.

Lastly, I would like to say that I have a dear aunt and uncle who have been faithful, devoted servants to the church here in the Portland area for over 60 years. They sent every one of their 8 children through St. Mary's, St. Cecelia's, and [or] Jesuit High School. They have surely tithed their income and their hearts faithfully for all those years. It grieves me to know that because of the church's unwillingness to honestly repent and remove these priests from active ministry and from the priesthood altogether, that the tithes of faithful servants like my aunt and uncle are being squandered on lawyers and the endless efforts to save face by covering the truth of what the Church is clearly guilty of. Severe action against these priests and new policies in place to protect children in the future are what the victims want more than financial compensation from the church. Unfortunately, the only thing we can see to do is to continue to [apply] financial pressure until the pain of it causes repentance and, most importantly, reform.

Appendix E
BETH'S MESSAGE TO JIM POOLE

Mr. Poole,

My name is Elizabeth Pierce. My mother was Martha Mueller. She was a lovely woman with 5 girls and 1 boy and a husband who was completely devoted to her. Martha fully embraced God and the Catholic Church. She believed, as was taught, that the priests were God's representatives on the earth. She raised all 6 children to revere and hold sacred the Church and the priest. When you, Mr. Poole, came into our family circle, it was with wicked, criminal intent. You may not see it that way, but a court of law has proven it true. You were the catalyst that tore our family apart. Your relationship with our mother took her to the brink of a living hell. I hold you responsible for our mother's death. All she ever believed about the sanctity of the Church was destroyed. She could not face her pain any longer; she took her life.

My 2 younger sisters, Mary and Roseanne, were 16 and 13 old [respectively when their mother died]. They were left motherless and had to bear the shame of suicide. After all, it was [taught that suicide is] a mortal sin. Roseanne had to keep secrets of your abuse buried in [her] heart for 40 years. I know my brother cannot talk about it. My life spun out of control. My heart was crushed; my emotions went numb. Tragic, regretful events took place in my life. Some of the outcome was due to your counsel to my mother. Our 2 oldest sisters, Joan and Diana, had to be affected but they do not feel comfortable to this day in sharing their thoughts [about these events] with me.

I believe you and I are the same in our humanity. We came into this world with original sin. The difference between us it this— when God came into my life in 1972, I repented of my sins and I gave my life to Him. You, Mr. Poole, have not repented of your sins. I cannot be your judge. God will be your judge. You will stand before Him soon. You will have to answer for every word, thought, and deed committed in your life.

I would like to read one of the parables that Jesus, His Hebrew name (Yeshua), taught and [was] recorded by Matthew chapter 13.

"The kingdom of heaven is like a man who sowed good seed in his field. But while everyone was sleeping, his enemy sowed weeds among the wheat, and went away. When the wheat sprouted and formed heads, then the weeds also appeared. The owner's servants came to him and said, 'Sir, didn't you sow good seed in your field? Where then did the weeds come from?'

"'An enemy did this,' he replied.

"The servants asked him, 'Do you want us to go and pull them up?'

"'No,' he answered, 'because while you are pulling the weeds, you may root up the wheat with them. Let both grow together until harvest. At that time I will tell the harvesters: First collect the weeds and tie them in bundles to be burned. Then gather the wheat and bring it into my barn.'

The disciples asked Jesus to explain the parable of the weeds in the field so he answered them, "The one who sowed the good seed is the Son of Man. The field is the world, and the good seeds stand for the sons of the kingdom. The weeds are the sons of the evil one, and the enemy who sows them is the devil. The harvest is the end of the age, and the harvesters are angels. As the weeds are pulled up and burned in the fire, so it will be at the end of the age. The Son of Man will send out his angels, and they will weed out of his kingdom everything that causes sin and all who do evil. They will throw them into the fiery furnace, where there will be weeping and gnashing of teeth. Then the righteous will shine like the sun in the kingdom of their Father. He who has ears, let him hear" (Matt. 13:24–29, 37–43 NIV).

There will be a day of reckoning for you, Mr. Poole. Where will you be? If you do not know, the answer is not hidden.

Appendix F
ROSEANNE'S PAPER ON HER
CHILDHOOD SEXUAL ABUSE

The best way to describe it [sexual abuse] is to say that when you are a little kid, you don't know what's normal and what's not. You don't understand right from wrong in terms of adult behavior. You only understand it in concrete ways, such as lying is bad, stealing is bad, and disobeying authority is bad. You don't know what sex is, and you don't know what the boundaries are of your own body with respect to the adults in your life who have authority over you.

You don't know what's right and what's wrong, but you feel it. You feel it in your body when someone violates you. When it's wrong it feels shameful, scary, even terrifying, and when those things are done to you by someone who is supposed to protect you and keep you safe, it throws your world into confusion. You don't have the abstract thinking skills to make sense of it or to be able to process it.

However, the human spirit and brain has a wonderful way of initiating a mechanism of self protection [*sic*] that helps you to survive the moment, but it is at the expense of the future. You don't know how to ascribe meaning to these events, so you don't. You set them aside and try to forget them, you retain the message to yourself that you should avoid having this happen to you again at all cost. But unfortunately, you don't have the ability the power or even the permission to protect yourself when it happens again. In fact, the message is that you are the one who is bad. When the priest tells you, you should like this, or that you must obey and cooperate, your internal instincts want to disobey, but you want to be a good person, an obedient, good Catholic girl. You don't want your mom to be disappointed in you or make the family look bad in front of the school or the church, or her family and friends.

So, you obey, you don't fight and you decide that there is something wrong with you for hating this, and for wanting to disobey. You decide that God must be very unhappy with you. You are too ashamed to talk to anyone about it, and you are ashamed to even talk to yourself about it, so you try very hard to forget the event, to forget the feeling, to forget the smell and the greasy hair, and the fingers in your vagina and your panties being pulled down, your dress being pulled up over your head, his hard penis pressed between your closed legs, against your vagina. Your mind goes blank and the fear takes you away to another place where things are quiet and where nothing bad is happening. You float above yourself and don't look down at what's happening, you look away and it [is] not there, he's not there, you are not there. You don't see the rest of what happens, so you don't even have to try to forget it.

But something brings you back and you are standing in the bathroom, he is angry with you, you did something really bad and don't know what it was, but he is washing your dress in the sink and telling you that you got it dirty and don't want your mother to know what you did to your dress, I don't know what I did to my dress, but it was really bad.

I now know that I will never go to heaven. This makes me very sad because I love God, and my mother and father love God, and God is good, but He is not for me. I don't get to go to heaven. I am only 7 years old and I am already so bad, I don't get to go to heaven....

The best way to describe this is to say that when you are a little kid, you don't know what's normal and what's not. Later in life you learn what is normal and right. No matter how much external knowledge you have about the world and other people, you can't really understand or know how much your experiences affected your life until you are brave enough to go back and face the fear. You must take your adult self back to your 7-year-old self and walk through it with her until she understands that she is not bad. That the world is safe, and that she can be loved.

Appendix G
THE GIRL AND THE GARDEN

I ncluded in the box that contained Dad's ledger, I also came across a packet of letters Dad had saved. The following is a copy of a letter he wrote to Roseanne in the late 1980s in response to her request for insight into Mom's mental illness and her request that he release Mom's medical records for her to read. Roseanne's original letter to Dad (very personal and too lengthy to include here) was simply signed "The Girl."

Dear Roseanne,

There was another girl I once knew. She was young, beautiful and intelligent. Her heart was full of Love Hope and Joy. It was a pleasure to know and be with a person like her.

We were married and it was good. We were known as the Ideal Couple and later, the Ideal Family. Our family was like a beautiful garden, full of beautiful flowers and sweet fruit.

What I didn't know was, there was a dark little cellar in her [Martha's] mind where she kept the seeds of past hurt feelings, disappointments and resentments. When she was alone she would visit the little cellar and deposit more seeds of hurt.

As time went on these seeds began to sprout. And she began to visit her garden in the cellar more often, staying there longer and longer each time, cultivating it and it grew. Then as it grew she would spend more time there and she neglected her garden in the light. And the weeds grew and the flowers wilted from lack of moisture and cultivation.

The garden in her cellar grew like a fungus and she began to live on it. It soured in her belly and she became sick and belched the bitterness, jealousy and hate from the cellar. They say she took her own life, but I say she died from the toxic fungus that she cultivated.

After her death I took the shoebox of letters from our closet shelf and could see that I held what was left of this dark garden. I started a hot fire in the fireplace and burned them One by One and prayed that no seed from that garden would find root in the garden of our family.

Dear Roseanne, Please cultivate your garden in the light where there is sunshine and fresh air and keep that cellar door Closed!

I Love You, Dad

Roseanne then wrote back:

Dear Dad,

I wanted you to know that I appreciated your letter and your insights as to the development of Mom's problems. I can understand your fears about that happening to me. However, I can assure you that my situation is very different. Rather than willingly succumbing to the dark places of self-pity and shame, I feel that my life has been a struggle to stay alive and to avoid the pitfalls into that place. The weeds grow up around me and I am constantly having to interrupt my otherwise happy life to stamp them out! If you only knew how hard I have strived, how much I try to suppress all that pain and hurt. I try to ignore the weeds, until at times they just overcome me. I have finally realized that they are irrepressible, that cutting them off at the tops does no good. I must once and for all get down on my hands and knees, as one does when weeding a beautiful flower bed, and dig them out by the roots once and for all. Oftentimes that disturbs the roots of the flowers and plants in the bed as well, I guess it can't be avoided, and it benefits them in the long run.

Right now I'm lost in a forest of weeds trying to find the shed with the garden tools in it. Thankfully God is slowly showing me the way.

Love, Roseanne

Resources

Support for caregivers and survivors of sexual abuse; Oregon

- http://oaasisoregon.org
- http://chrysaliscounseling.net/individual-counseling/learn-more-about-child-sexual-abuse

National Organizations for caregivers and survivors of sexual abuse

- http://www.nsvrc.org/sites/default/files/nsvrc_publications_resource-list_online-resources-for-survivors.pdf
- http://www.nctsn.org/resources/audiences/parents-caregivers/understanding-child-traumatic-stress
- http://www.snapnetwork.org
- http://www.netgrace.org
- http://www.road-to-recovery.org
- http://bishopaccountability.org
- http://www.usccb.org/issues-and-action/child-and-youth-protection/charter.cfm

Drug and alcohol abuse; recovery and support:

- http://www.samhsa.gov
- https://www.na.org
- http://www.aa.org
- http://www.al-anon.org (support for friends and family of substance abusers)

Suicide Support; Prevention, Survivors of a loved one's suicide, Suicide attempt survivors

- http://www.suicidology.org/About-AAS
- http://www.allianceofhope.org

Mental health resources

- https://www.nami.org
- http://www.samhsa.gov

Elsie Boudreau, founder of Arctic – Winds Healing Winds, Native Alaskan:

A victim herself and now an advocate for victims of clergy abuse: https://www.facebook.com/Arctic-Winds-Healing-Winds-1556187191282847

Books

- *Getting Past Your Past* by Francine Shapiro PhD.
- *The Courage to Heal* by Ellen Bass and Laura Davis
- *Surviving Survival* by Laurence Gonzalez
- *Why People Die by Suicide* by Thomas Joiner
- *Breaking Free* by Beth Moore

Films and Movies

- Interview with Elsie Boudreau: http://www.ktuu.com/news/news/movie-spotlights-clergy-abuse/36958430

- PBS documentary featuring Elsie Bourdreau's quest for healing and justice: http://www.pbs.org/wgbh/pages/frontline/the-silence
- Deliver Us From Evil, by Oliver O'Grady
- Spotlight: http://spotlightthefilm.com

194 | My Father's Ledger

Notes

Preface
1. Lyle Lofgren, "Babes in the Woods,"
http://www.lizlyle.lofgrens.org/RmOlSngs/RTOS-
BabesWood.html. Originally from *Inside Bluegrass*, January 2001,
accessed February 5, 2015.

Chapter One
1. Phillip Yancey, *What's So Amazing About Grace?* (Grand
Rapids, MI: Zondervan, 1997), 89–90.

Chapter Five
1. Ashbel S. Green, "Sex-abuse suits embroil Jesuits in
Northwest," The Oregonian. Monday, November 14, 2005.
Associated Press, "Several Northwest Jesuits facing sex-abuse
lawsuits." Portland [Oregon] [The Bend Oregon] Bulletin Tuesday,
November 15, 2005.

Chapter Six
1. Father Duffy was also a Jesuit priest who became a family
friend and was like a "kind brother" to our mother. He raped
Roseanne one day when he was alone with her, on our parents' bed
while "babysitting." She was eight years old at the time. He passed
away in 1992.
2. There is a prophetic irony to this as we would eventually receive
copies of our mother's medical records, 450 pages accrued over a
six-year period. Now that was voluminous!

Chapter Thirteen
1. I discovered later that Oregon was one of the few states at that
time that allowed fifteen-year-olds to legally marry, as long as they
had parental consent.

Chapter Fourteen
1. Bill W. and Sam Shoemaker, *The Big Book*, 164. The founder of
AA, along with Shoemaker, wrote this book to help the addict
become "happily and usefully whole."

Chapter Fifteen

1. Ironically, one of the attorneys who appeared in this documentary played a key role in eventually helping settle Roseanne's case.
2. The Davenport Hotel and Tower, Spokane Washington, accessed August 28, 2012, http://www.thedavenporthotel.com/history.

Chapter Nineteen

1. Timothy L. Sanford, *I Have to Be Perfect: And other Parsonage Heresies* (Llama Pr, 1998), quoted in Chonda Pierce, *It's Always Darkest Before the Fun Comes Up* (Grand Rapids, MI: Zondervan, 1998) 95.
2. For a complete explanation of this teaching, go to http://4laws.com.

About Mary A. Mills

After raising two sons and enjoying a successful career as a Health and Fitness Professional, Mary moved from the busy suburbs of Portland Oregon to a log cabin at the end of a long country road in Montana's Bitterroot Valley – Her dreams of a loving relationship, living in the country and riding horseback on mountain trails, fulfilled beyond her wildest imaginings. Shortly after her big move, Mary began a new career as a Massage Therapist, opening a private practice, which will soon to be celebrating a 20  year anniversary. She is now enjoying her most exciting adventure yet, as a Builder/Author; the Builder of a Grace Filled Legacy. It is Mary's prayer that her story, as told through the pages of *My Father's Ledger*, inspire you to Dare to Hope for *your* own life story to be made anew.

Building a Legacy of Grace

And they shall rebuild the old ruins, They shall raise up the former desolations...the desolations of many generations.
Isaiah 61:4 NKJV

Build: To develop of form (something) gradually.

Rebuild: To build (something) again after it has been damaged or destroyed, to make important improvements or changes in (something)

Legacy: Something transmitted by or received from an ancestor or predecessor or from the past.

Contact Information

To learn more about Mary A. Mills, to find out about her current and future writing projects, or to inquire about booking a speaking engagement:

Email her at: contact@maryamills.com

Visit her website: www.MaryAMills.com where you can sign up for her bi-monthly, *Building a Legacy of Grace* newsletter.

Like her on Facebook at: Facebook.com/Mary-A-Mills-Building-a-Legacy-of-Grace-17038153333682

Made in the USA
San Bernardino, CA
20 September 2017